Five GI's in Battle

- World War II -

George Hudson Wirth

Hud

Five GI's in Battle - World War II -
George Hudson Wirth
Copyright © 2001 by GHW Books

Published by:

GHW Books
NorthBrook, IL 60062

ISBN: 0-9715939-0-6
Book and cover design by Brian Arthur Blevins
Date of publication: (10/23/01)

This book was manufactured in the United States of America.

This book is dedicated to

John Howard Axelson

and to the hundreds of thousands of young
American soldiers, sailors, marines, and airmen
who didn't make it home from World War II.

Table of Contents

Preface

Bibliography

PREFACE

Why write more about World War II? Historians and scholars have written great books about this era – 1939-1945. We can go to any library in the USA and find excellent works on this subject – especially about those people who governed, planned and managed the war efforts of both sides of this enormous struggle to save the world from totalitarianism. But, these are not the ones who actually fought. We have read that during this six year period about 50 million people died – yes, 50 million although we will never know the exact figure! Most of the people were civilians including the six million Jews exterminated in the Holocaust. This era is arguably the worst time in world history – man destroying his fellow man systematically.

I think Americans would like to know more about the lives of those soldiers who were in close combat. It has been a privilege to conduct taped oral interviews with these friends of mine – these "Citizen Soldiers", as Stephen Ambrose would call them. Their human interest stories are their memoirs for future generations and history scholars. Of course, some came home from the war to their families and wanted to forget and get on with their lives. And tragically, some didn't come home. I can only write about the soldiers that I knew in World War II and where I have access to information from military records to verify dates, place etc. The 50th Armored Infantry Battalion (*1000 men*) was part of the 6th Armored Division (*10,000 men*) that was one of the divisions in Gen. George Patton's Third Army in Europe. It landed on Utah beach in July of 1944 after there was room for and the need for armored divisions in the Normandy breakout against German defenses. It fought from Normandy through to the Mulde River near the Chemnitz – Leipzig - Dresden area in Germany waiting for the Russians to meet them in late April 1945. The official 6th Armored Division history, *The Super Sixth* - 1975, written by Prof. George F. Hoffman lists the casualties in the 1000 man 50th Armored Infantry Battalion – 213 men and officers killed in action, 829 wounded in action and 3 missing in action for a total of 1045 battle casualties – more than 100 per cent. That is why the battalion needed replacements – all young , most of them eighteen and nineteen years old! Very, very few of the infantry battalion soldiers lasted through the whole campaign. The odds were against you. Clarence Sanning, First Sergeant of our Company B, said, " We were a different group at the end of the war than when we sailed to Europe."

1

American soldiers, sailors, airmen and marines fought this war around the world – the Atlantic Ocean, Africa, Europe, Asia and the Pacific Ocean. It could be said that the world today might be radically different had not the United States used its manpower and industrial power to help the Allies. Imagine for yourself what might the world be like if we had stayed as an isolationist nation as we were in the 1930's? What if President Franklin D. Roosevelt hadn't pushed us toward re-armament in 1940 with peacetime conscription of men? What about the Lend Lease act to give Great Britain 50 old US destroyers to bolster their Navy in 1940? After all, England was fighting the Nazis alone when France fell in June 1940. Then on June 22, 1941, after Hitler invaded Russia, we Americans poured more supplies into convoys going to Great Britain and also to Murmansk to aid the Russians in their attempt to halt the Panzer Armies. Particularly, after Pearl Harbor, December 7,1941, the American people rolled up their sleeves and accomplished an unbelievable job to help win the war! What would have happened if Hitler had won the war or the two enemies, Germany and Russia, governed by the Stalin regime, had made peace? The what ifs could go on and on. A strong case can be made that without the help and sacrifice of the American people in World War II, our world society would be considerably less free than it is today.

It is important to understand that fighting in World War II was very different from all previous wars. Weaponry was more sophisticated – more powerful, accurate in range and extremely more deadly. Trench warfare was gone after World War I. Mass attacks similar to "over the top" were also gone – except for the D-Day invasion in Normandy June 6, 1944, landings in the Italian campaign and the invasions of islands in the Pacific theater. Once ashore, GI's had to fight like Cowboys and Indians and whenever possible get below ground level and into foxholes – especially at nighttime. Any bunching of troops lead to deadly artillery shells and shrapnel. Open exposure in the daytime brought machine gun or sniper fire from a hidden enemy position. Tank warfare brought fast mobile artillery into position quickly. American gunfire from dusk to dawn exposed soldiers' positions or locations of artillery pieces to the enemy because of the muzzle flash.

GI's rarely knew other soldiers in their Company (*200 men*) other than those in their own platoon (*50 men*) or their rifle squad (*12 men*). Their closest buddies were their own rifle squad members who relied upon each other to survive. When attacking the enemy, infantrymen were taught to spread out and then leap frog ahead in small groups of two, three or four soldiers at a time, hitting the ground quickly seeking any depression that would give any kind of temporary shelter – a furrow in a plowed field, a ditch, perhaps a tree, a house, a stone wall. They fired their semi-automatic M-1 Garand rifles from the prone or kneeling position to cover the next group moving forward. Perhaps the most important part of combat to recognize regarding American troops was that they were almost always in the attack mode versus a defensive position. The one big exception in Europe was the beginning of the Battle of the Bulge, in the Ardennes - December 16, 1944 to January 28, 1945. From January 1, 1945 on, they were on the attack again even there. In order to attack, a soldier must leave his temporary shelter. The enemy is positioned in a hidden place, in the ground, a bunker, a pillbox, a village house or building, behind a hedgerow or a stone wall and sometimes a small stream or river. It is obvious that the attacker has more exposure to wounds or death than the defense. To make up for this inequity, the American military used more artillery, equipment, air power and motorized armor speed to offset the defense and they needed more replacements.

When the American Army was refitting their units after the Battle of the Bulge, the German Army hunkered down behind their Siegfried line (*as Americans called it*) or Westwall. To give a perspective of how spread out front line troops were sometimes, the 6th Armored Division occupied a front of about 15 miles long looking into the bunkers of the Westwall. Most of the line was held by two Armored Infantry battalions (*either the 9th, 44th or 50th*) of 1000 men each with one of the three battalions in reserve. Imagine spreading 2000 men over a distance of 8 miles? One can see that only scattered small units would be in the foxholes at strategic locations along the entire front. This was typical of Army units getting ready for the next big push into the Rhineland and Ruhr and Central Germany toward the Russian Army driving to the west.

I have a friend, Colonel Jim Moncrief, who can describe problems of the fighting soldier better than anyone! He is the oldest living member and the highest remaining officer who was on the General Staff of the 6th Armored Division in World War II. This is his distinguished background. He was born June 7, 1912 in Manchester Georgia. He graduated from the University of Georgia in 1933 as a 2nd Lieutenant, Infantry Reserve. He was on active duty in the CCC (*Civilian Conservation Corps*) 1933-34. In February

1941, he was called to active duty at Ft. Benning, Georgia and then transferred to the 6th Armored Division a year later in 1942 – just after Pearl Harbor. He served with the 6th Armored throughout the war from beginning to end. He was a Lt. Colonel, Chief of Staff of the 6th Armored Division upon deactivation in 1945. Col. Jim spent a career in the military including stints as Professor of Military Science and Tactics at both the Universities of West Virginia and Wisconsin. He retired as a full Colonel in 1965 with many decorations. He has written several books and is a World War II historian in his own right! Last year at the final 6th Armored Division Association reunion in Louisville, Kentucky, at the spry age of eighty-eight, he gave a marvelous final banquet speech to a crowd of 1400 veterans and guests. The Association disbanded because all the veterans in 2001 are in their late 70's, 80's and 90's and we will all be history shortly.

Here are excerpts from *Close Combat or Eye-Ball to Eye-Ball With the Enemy* by James S. Moncrief Jr. with his permission.

" It is known that certain soldiers have tougher jobs than others. The guy that is a typist or clerk in Theater Headquarters certainly has a far easier life than the ammunition carrier in a mortar squad of an Infantry outfit. The fellow standing guard at the entrance into Corps Headquarters bivouac is not subjected to the rigors of combat as is the rifleman of an Infantry squad. The experience of the truck driver moving supplies from the rear echelon to the Field Army "dumps" can't be compared to that of the tank driver, who suddenly finds his tank face to face with an enemy tank as he makes his turn at a road intersection. The radio operator at the G-3 tent of a Division Headquarters enjoys comforts and conveniences never experienced by a machine gunner on a half-track. The cook in an Infantry Battalion Headquarters does not face the enemy's rifle and machine gun fire as does the rifleman of an Infantry squad.

Yes, the job of being a soldier who faces the enemy eye ball to eye ball should be singled out as being the toughest, the most dangerous, with greater risks of life, the least comfortable and requiring the most physical endurance than any assignment in the Army. He may be an Infantry rifleman, who, while facing enemy fire, advances with his fellow platoon members to knock out a machine gun at the top of the hill. He could be a member of a tank crew as his tank gets in a more advantageous position to fire at an enemy tank emerging from the woods. He could be an engineer racing onto a bridge to

4

cut wires leading to an explosive, which the enemy, in his retreat, had installed to detonate the bridge. He may be an Artillery Forward Observer, positioned in the church steeple, who is, by radio, bringing fire from the heavy guns to bear on an enemy advancing within fifty yards of the church, and the area occupied by friendly troops.

In addition to the extremely hazardous conditions of enemy fire faced by the Close Combat Soldier, he is constantly subjected to personal hardships, far more serious than those experienced by other soldiers. He is forced to live with: hazardous weather conditions, cold food, little sleep, no baths for days, maybe weeks, little chance for a change of clothing. Because of the elements of Mother Nature he endures: the snow, the ice, the rain, and ankle-deep mud, while in clothing wet to the skin. Much of the time he operates from the cramped and limited space of a narrow, hastily constructed foxhole, which he has dug, sometimes into the frozen ground, but always with a small inadequate hand shovel. Frequently, the foxhole is dug while he is under fire from the enemy.

The casualty level of these types of soldiers is much higher than among others. In most units where Close Combat was a daily routine, the casualty rate was over 100%. Being a replacement assigned to such a unit engaged in Close Combat has to be one of the worst experiences to which a human being can be exposed. Nothing can produce a feeling more awkward, insecure, humbling, and sensitive; and at the same time generate so little gratification, appreciation or understanding. Therefore, the Replacements who join a unit where " eye-ball to eye-ball" soldering is routine deserve double credit or recognition.

For a nation to be victorious at war, those soldiers in close combat with the enemy must be successful…. Such can not be accomplished without routing the enemy forces from his position on the ground….the various activities of the Command and Staff functions of each of the seven or eight echelon levels (*from Company, Battalion, Regiment, Division, Corps, Army, Army Group, to Theater*) of command in a Theater of Operations are centered and focused on insuring that the soldiers in close combat with the enemy accomplish their mission….

… The Combat Infantryman's badge is given across the board to all members of an Infantry Regiment or Battalion… Not every soldier in an Infantry Regiment or Battalion is subjected to the eye-ball to eye-ball combat. It is my opinion that the Army should create a new Decoration called the "Close Combat Medal" to award soldiers not restricted to Infantrymen, who perform their duties under conditions of "eye-ball" contact with the enemy. Further, I believe the Replacement Soldier who earns the Close Combat Medal should receive additional special recognition."

Why was World War II fought by the Americans? The answer might be better expressed by some French people who had first hand knowledge of occupation by the Nazis in their own country. I met a very interesting French gentleman in the year 2000 – Georges Lecourt. He is now the Roman Catholic Chaplain at the St. Lo prison and fluent in English. Early in 1939, he attended a special school in England and then later taught English in France. He was born on a farm near Avranches in Normandy south of St. Lo.

In June 1940, just before Marshall Petain signed the armistice with Germany, Georges was working in their farm hayfield when he heard a tremendous explosion in the distance. It was the FFI blowing up a German ammunition and supply train. His father had him hitch up their horse and drive toward St. Lo to see what merchandise they might scavenge. Among their salvage were French Army boots which the Germans had confiscated.

He heard about D-Day, June 6, 1944, while he was in school. Georges was seventeen years old then. They dismissed school to give students and their families time to decide what to do. Since they lived on a farm away from St. Lo, the largest city in the area, his family was not in much danger. They decided to stay on their farm. On the evening of D-Day the Allies started bombing larger towns – some 22 miles south of the Normandy beaches to harass supplies coming to the Germans.

Georges said the underground in Normandy mostly gathered information. Very little damage was done to German property or trains for fear of immediate reprisal - the firing squad. He told the story of the French painter working in German headquarters who managed to steal a copy of the map showing details of every defensive position along the Normandy coast. So, the Allies knew every German bunker and gun location.

During the German occupation of France 1940-1944, the German attitude toward the French people was much more tolerant than the Nazi treatment of other nationalities – especially the Russians. As long as you were not Jewish or as long as you were not earmarked as part of the French FIS , you were pretty much left alone. During these four years, German soldiers were billeted in his farm home – similar to many French families in his area forced to provide a bedroom. While they were not welcomed at first, they came to know the young German soldiers, most of whom were polite. They lived there with the family, coming home each day or night from their military duties. Sometimes families got attached to the young soldiers who treated them well and showed them pictures of their families back in Germany. Even today, some French families stay in touch with surviving Germans.

I asked Georges how the French in Normandy felt about American soldiers. After all, before Americans arrived, rural French got along quite well. Farmers had food from their gardens. Their villages were not damaged, homes were intact. As long as they followed the rules, Germans treated them pretty well. D-Day, June 6, 1944 changed the whole Normandy scene. In his sector of Normandy, American artillery shelled small towns to desolation. The Air Force bombed cities to obliteration. During the Normandy campaign, over ten thousand French civilians were killed – to say nothing of the wounded and displaced families. Georges said, " The French people hated the Nazi regime! The Americans were our liberators and our heroes. We were willing to pay. This was the price of war. We French wanted our freedom more than anything! We shall never be grateful enough to Americans who came to liberate us!"

Another French lady, Martine Gripari, a tour guide in Normandy said it well, " We are accustomed to war. We have had wars for at least a thousand years dating back to William the Conqueror in 1066 when he invaded England – the Battle of Hastings. We were willing to suffer – losing our cities and our people in order to be a free France!"

Americans soldiers today coming to Normandy are treated like heroes. At the Omaha Beach American cemetery, there are 9,387 soldiers buried (*including 307 unknown soldiers*) in this immaculately cared for National Monument – rows upon rows of white crosses. It is a touching scene, visited by thousands of people each year to pay respect to these fallen GI's who made the supreme sacrifice to free the world.

Not far away, at the German cemetery of La Cambe, 21,202 soldiers are buried. Most Germans were buried where they fell – others were exhumed and were buried in large cemeteries like La Cambe. Dr. Jean-Pierre Benamou, curator of the D-Day museum in Bayeux, said that after 56 years, they continue to find 12-20 new bodies per year from farmers plowing their fields or digging for new construction. Germans come to visit the cemeteries and see the graves, but they know they are not very welcome by the French in Normandy. They keep to themselves and live mostly in trailer camps.

These two cemeteries, in a quiet sobering setting in Normandy, depict the futility of war – mans' inhumanity to his fellow man. You can not leave these cemeteries without hope for peace in a better world for generations to come. This book tells the stories of a few "Close Combat" American soldiers and the pain they and their families suffered in helping to bring this war to an end. They are a few of the hundreds of thousands of heroes and European liberators our French friends talked about.

WILBUR "WEB" MAGNUS HALVORSEN

Web grew up in Austin on the west side of Chicago. He was born Sept. 18, 1918-just before Armistice Day of World War I which was November 11, 1918. Web's family heritage was Norwegian. His father, Christian Halvorsen, was born in Norway and came to America in 1884 with his mother when he was 9 years old. Christian was one of a large family of twelve children. Grandfather, Bertran Halvorsen, a Norwegian sailor and fisherman, had come earlier to Chicago working on the ships in Lake Michigan. When he had saved enough money, he sent for his wife and family, just like many immigrant families of that era in the late 1800's.

Web's mother, Olga also came from Norway. Her brother, Dr. Magnus (*he shortened his Norwegian name from Magnussen like many immigrants of the time*), living in the Rogers Park area of Chicago, sent for his younger sister, Olga in 1909. She was 26 years old at the time and got a job working for Web's grandmother. Web said that she spoke no English at that time and after she learned it, she always had a slight accent. She was an accomplished pianist and played at numerous Norwegian gatherings. Her husband to be, Christian, had a very fine voice and sang along with the accompanist, so the two fell in love and were married in 1911.

Their first child, a little girl -Marion was born in 1913. Three years later a boy, Don, arrived in 1916. Along came their youngest child, Wilbur in 1918. Christian was a salesman for the Gold Star Oil Co. in Chicago. The family had a very nice home on

Thomas Street with a large contingent of Norwegians in the area. His father was active in community affairs and was instrumental in raising funds for building the Austin YMCA. Web said his family survived the Great Depression years, 1929-1940, pretty well. His Dad had a good job, they had a car and enough income to live a comfortable family life.

Web attended the John Hay elementary school and graduated from Austin High School in 1937. His school years were during the depth of the Depression, 25-30 % unemployment, soup kitchens, major bankruptcies, bank closings, etc. Yet, people came to the Windy City by the thousands to see the Chicago Worlds Fair of 1933-1934. The fair was a break from reality in world politics. At the same time, Adolph Hitler became Chancellor of Germany in 1932 (without a majority of the vote). Through Nazi terror, he subdued any German opposition to his regime. In the meantime, the United States was struggling through the Depression years -- another war coming along was incomprehensible to Americans. We had become an isolationist society with a downsized Army ranked <u>sixteenth</u> in the world – thinking the oceans would protect us.

After graduating from Austin High School in 1937, Web was invited to drive to St. Olaf College in Northfield, Minnesota with a neighbor family to visit their son. Web immediately decided that this where he'd like to attend college. Room, board and tuition was $ 350 per year and his family could afford the money. Web loved his time at this excellent Norwegian school in the small farmland town made famous by the Jesse James gang raid in the 1870's. He was captain of the wrestling team and especially liked the local rivalry with Carleton College which is in the same town across the Cannon River. He graduated in June 1941 with a BA degree in Economics.

In 1940, what was happening in America? From the Feb. 14th,1940 issue of *Life* magazine, the following articles and advertisements give us an idea of the times:

A 1940 Chevrolet 4 door sedan sold for $659 dollars.
Women school teachers average salary was $1200 per year.
Steinway grand piano sold for $985 dollars.
At 19 years old, Mickey Rooney was the most popular actor in Hollywood.
Kaiser Wilhelm was 81 years old.
The Finns were defeating the Russians in the frozen north woods of Finland.

The magazine was full of cigarette and liquor ads.
First photos of the British aircraft carrier, Courageous, sunk in Sept. 1939 by U-boats with two torpedoes in 7 minutes - 701 men lost.

President Franklin Delano Roosevelt was elected to a third term in office in 1940. He pushed for a peacetime conscription law in 1940 to mobilize an Army. World War II had erupted when the Nazi's invaded Poland in September 1939. The Lend Lease Law had been enacted by Congress in 1941. The USA received leases on several British naval bases in the Atlantic in exchange for 50 old destroyers to help England fight the Germans after the fall of France in June 1940. The British Army, of 337,000 soldiers, were pinned to the northern coast of France at Dunkirk. They were rescued by a huge fleet of ships including every small boat available on the English coast. Eight hundred craft, piloted by civilians and Navy, evacuated them over the last days of May until June 3, 1940. The majority of the British army escaped without their equipment These world shaking events took place during Web's junior year at college. The Allies did not return in force to the Continent until D-Day, June 6, 1944, four years later.

" After graduation, I took a few weeks off and started looking for a job," Web said. " In those years, I'll tell you, jobs were hard to come by! They weren't paying anything. Even with a college education, they were paying $18.50 per week. Finally, I settled for a job with the Morton Salt Co. for $21.00 a week", added Web. Describing his job, "I took the Lake Street El to the loop where I worked in the office in various departments. They were grooming me to handle their automobile fleet - keeping the salesmen's cars in order."

He worked for Morton Salt Co. until he got his " Greetings" from the President of the United States and his friends and neighbors – his draft notice - to report for duty on October 31,1942.- Halloween ! It said, " …you are hereby notified that you have now been selected for training and service in the Army." Further at the bottom it read, "Willful failure to report promptly to this Local Board at the hour and the day named in this notice is a violation of the Selective Training and Service Act of 1940 and subjects the violator to fine and imprisonment".

After being inducted at Ft. Sheridan, IL, on the north shore of Chicago, he was sent to Camp Polk, Louisiana where Armored divisions were training. His basic training was with the 7th Armored Division for eight weeks of infantry training. " They put us on a train to California for desert training." Web continues his story. " After about three weeks, the First Sergeant came in one morning and said the Company Commander wanted to see me. The first thing I thought, was what did I do now? When I got to his tent, I recognized quite a few other men in the company. I was told they were going to start up a cadre for Camp Polk (*near Leesville, Louisiana*). I was kicked up from a Private to a buck Sergeant, (*buck means the lowest rank level a three striper*). We were told not to

waste any time – to go pack our gear. In that Spring of 1943, they put us on a train and shipped us back to Camp Polk where I didn't want to be. Boy! that Summer was hot! The only relief we got was at the Sergeants club where they had an air conditioner and there weren't a lot of them."

Web at Camp Polk 1942

Web stayed there as cadre *(meaning training new troops)* until December 1943. He said, " We were told to pack our gear and we were going west again. I remember we used company money along the way to buy fresh beef that we had for Christmas dinner on the train .We landed near Lompoc, California at Camp Cooke." It was here that Web joined the 6th Armored Division and was assigned to Company A of the 50th Armored Infantry Battalion. He was made a Staff Sergeant (*three stripes above and one below*) a notch higher in rank but still a rifle squad leader of twelve soldiers.

In a short time the 6th Armored Division packed up and headed for the east coast by train – with all their armored vehicles. This division had to get to England before D-Day for further training. Armored divisions were scheduled to land on the Normandy beaches as soon as there was room for them. The breakthrough was planned after a hole in the German defensive positions was opened. There was much to do in organizing operation Overlord – D-Day.

Father, Christian; Mother, Olga and Web 1943

Web got a furlough home to say goodbye to his family. Every family that saw their young men leave for overseas duty wondered if they would ever see them again – or if they did get back home would they be whole! It was an emotional goodbye!

There were a few days in New York before embarking on ships to carry them to the British Isles. Web told a " Hollywood " type story about his friend, Lt. Alfred Newman who was his Company A commander(*an infantry company is composed of four rifle platoons of 48 men along with a heavy weapons platoon-200 to 250 men*). He went to the big New York USO canteen where most of the GI's stopped, - that is if they were able to get a pass before embarkation. Lt. Al met this lovely young lady, Kitty, and it was love at first sight! Al and Kitty only saw each other a few days in New York. They stayed in touch during the war by mail. Lieutenant Al Newman (later made Captain) was wounded in action. After he returned to the USA, they were married, enjoying a long happy life together until he passed away in the late 1990's.

February 6,1944, the 6th Armored joined what was the largest convoy in history heading for England. The whole 50th Armored Infantry Battalion (1000 men and their equipment) boarded the USS Henrico for the trip to Grenoc, Scotland arriving February 21st. By train they traveled to Burford, England where they settled down. Burford, Oxfordshire, is 65 miles northwest of the center of London. Before D-Day, there were more than 2 million U.S soldiers in England – most in the southern parts. The standard joke was that England would tip into the sea with all this weight.

While the division had trained hard in the USA and England, it was not <u>all</u> work and <u>no </u>play! Web and his good friend, Sgt. Jim Johnson, also a rifle squad leader in the same platoon, decided to go into town their first weekend in England. They changed out of their fatigues and put on their uniforms, headed down the hill into this beautiful town of Burford. Web continues, "We went into the first pub and it was loaded with GI's. These two gals in uniforms, they were sitting in the back on a stepped-up platform where we could see them. We maneuvered our way up to them, got talking to them and had some warm English beer.

We visited with them until the pub closed – all English pubs closed at 10 o'clock. Of course, when we got out it was pitch dark. We walked the girls, who were sisters, home and they invited us in. Their names were Edith (Edie) and Bobbie Search. We met their mother and father and they didn't have much to share but they shared a little meat sandwich with us. That was our first contact with them.

The next day we met them and their brother and they had bicycles for us , so we bicycled all afternoon. That evening we went back to the pub and played some darts. There happened to be a piano, so I sat down at the piano and started playing." Web told how he learned to play the piano. When he was a teenager, he'd sometimes listen to the radio, WGN, to hear a man play the piano. He sold programs for $1.75 that guaranteed to teach you how to play by ear in seven easy lessons. Web sent his money in and learned to play. He continued his story, " Pretty soon I had a whole gang around the piano. We were singing all the old songs I could think of – *"Down by the Old Mill Stream", "You Are My Sunshine", "Roll Out the Barrel", "Roll Me Over In the Clover", "Let Me Call You Sweatheart"* and *"I've Been Working On the Railroad"* and any more they wanted to hear. It gave all the soldiers a lift. The girls had to get back on duty the next day. They only got back home once or twice a month. They had stories to tell but you had to pump it out of them. They were serving in an anti-aircraft battery in Portsmouth. One time I asked Edie, 'How did you do this past week? ' She replied, ' I did all right but Bobbie did real good last night she shot down four planes!' Bobbie responded, 'Well Edie did OK she got a couple ,too!'

The girls became their English girlfriends. The weekends they were not home, Mr. and Mrs. Search invited them to stay with them in Burford. Web adds, " In the meantime we stayed in their beds – nice clean sheets – a good mattress – and their little granddaughter, Valerie, bringing tea to us in the morning. They took us in like their own sons! Mr. Search was badly wounded in World War I - shrapnel in his back. He was the town air raid warden and made sure the town was completely blacked out for air raid safety."

This photo, with their daughters and the soldiers, was sent to Mr. and Mrs. Halvorsen in Chicago by the Search family. A note on the back reads, " To Mr. & Mrs. Halvorsen with all our best wishes from us in England G H Search."

From left: Sgt. Jim Johnson, Edith Search, Bobbie Search, Sgt. Web Halvorsen, Gladys, the oldest sister and her little daughter, Valerie.

The 6th Armored Division was not going to spend the war in England. D-Day on June 6, 1944 set the armor in motion. The time in England was spent putting all their vehicles, tanks, half-tracks, artillery and all other equipment in top working order.

The battle plan of Eisenhower and Montgomery was executed – but at a much slower pace than had been expected. The heroic action of the British and Canadians on Gold, Juno and Sword beaches on the Normandy coast accomplished much but they did not take their D-Day objective, Caen, a city of 60,000 people – some 6 miles inland – until July.

American casualties landing at Omaha and Utah beaches were much higher than expected. The American plans for the 1st and 29th Infantry Division landings at Omaha went awry. Like the Colonel in England said after being briefed for D-Day, " You can take these plans and throw them away, once the battle starts." Aircraft were supposed to saturate bomb the beach landing areas. It was partially overcast and cloudy. 600 tons of bombs dropped on the nearby village of the Longues-sur-Mer battery, missing all the German bunkers and gun emplacements. Naval gun fire from battleships and cruisers had the task of knocking out the heavy German guns in huge concrete bunkers. They were successful on some beaches, especially in the British sector. The seas were heavy and the ship-roll placed most shots well inland from the target zone. Follow up artillery from destroyers was planned to clean up the German positions. Most of the Navy observation officers were killed or wounded going in with the first waves of infantry soldiers. In addition their radios got wet – they didn't work - so they could not give fire directions to their ships. The gunnery officers aboard were afraid to fire not knowing how far inland the GI'S were located. They were pinned down on the beach!

The result was a disaster at Omaha. 2000 Americans were killed at Omaha the first day of the landings, to say nothing of the wounded. It was chaos! The movie, "Saving Private Ryan" depicts the horror of the Omaha beach landings. At one point in the morning, Gen. Omar Bradley was considering moving the balance of the follow-up troops to the Utah beach area to the west where the casualties were much lower. He couldn't face leaving the survivors of the first few waves alone on Omaha. The heroic action by a few infantrymen and their non-coms and officers, to scale the bluffs behind Omaha, knocking out German gun emplacements from the rear, saved the day. Many D-Day soldiers are buried in the beautiful American Military cemetery above Omaha Beach where there are 9,387 white cross graves (including, 307 unknown soldiers).

In the meantime the 6th Armored Division was awaiting its turn for combat. The Allies had made very little progress advancing except for the capture of the Cherbourg peninsula and its' harbor June 30th by the American 4th Infantry Division, which had landed at Utah beach. The invasion forces were essentially hemmed into a narrow beach area from Caen on the east for some 50 miles west. They needed room for the armored troops and equipment. The Americans needed a breakthrough of the German positions in order to get the Armor in terrain where they are efficient. On July 25th near St. Lo, the breakthrough came – but not until after the American Air Corps mistakenly bombed the 30th Infantry Division killing about 400 Americans including Lt. Gen. Lesley Mc Nair, the highest ranking American officer killed in Europe. Thereafter, Gen. Bradley prohibited any further high level bombings by the Strategic Air Command, allowing only Tactical Air Command low level bombers to assist ground troops.

6th Armored Division leading elements disembarked on July 18th at Utah beach and by July 25th the last of personnel and material were ashore. Gen. George Patton's

3rd US Army was formed by August 1st, with the 10,000 soldier 6th Armored division a part of it. Web's unit, the 50th Armored Infantry Battalion was one of three, one thousand man infantry units in the division – the others being the 9th & 44th Inf. Battalions.

How much equipment is in an Armored division?:

168 - Sherman medium tanks, ;

83 - Light tanks,

54 - M-7 Artillery 105mm howitzers

547 - Half-tracks ;

36   Tank destroyers

81   Recon armored cars

509   Trucks 2 ½ ton-

551   Jeeps

8   L-5 Piper Cub spotter airplanes

It's no wonder it took several days to disembark 2029 vehicles at Utah beach!

After the American Army broke through the German lines at St. Lo, Patton sent his two armored divisions, the 6th and the 4th crashing south toward the Brittany peninsula. The 6th Armored moved out on July 27th and advanced south 26 miles to Avranches the first day of combat. The original strategy plan aimed to seal off the port of Brest, capture the nearby U-boat pens and open a shipping supply port for the mountains of supplies needed. The 6th Armored turned east, was given orders to avoid and bypass resistance and race some 200 miles to the west toward Brest. This drive was made without any flank support – only tactical fighter and bomber aircraft to seal off the flanks from German attacks. By August 2nd the advance was well under way. The French FFI, the resistance, had now come out into the open assisting the division as guides and informants of German positions.

As the armored columns dashed toward Brest, attempting to bypass German resistance, they were continually bothered by sniper fire. Woe be to the Germans caught as snipers and turned over to the FFI. Often they were shot without any mercy!

Time after time, passing through the small French villages, the GI's were greeted as conquering heroes by the men, women and children. Flowers were tossed at the moving vehicles, flags waved and occasionally a person would run out with a bottle of the local calvados or wine. They were celebrating their liberation from four years of Nazi occupation – even though many of their homes and families were destroyed by the invading American Army. The French loved their American liberators!

By August 7th, the 6th had reached the outskirts of the German defense system outside Brest. It was expected to be garrisoned with about 4000 enemy soldiers. Unknown to G-2, the intelligence unit of the division, Brest had been reinforced by German Infantry replacements from the Crozon peninsula and now stood at 20,000 troops in a semi-circle around the port. On August 8th, Lt. Col. Ernest Mitchell entered the city of Brest in a Jeep flying a white flag demanding the surrender of the garrison. The German commander refused – under the orders from Hitler to fight to the last man!

In the meantime, the 266th German Infantry division in retreat from the breakthrough near Avranches, bumped into the rear of the 6th Armored division attacking its' supply trains (*not rail trains but military truck supply columns*). Maj. Gen. Robert W. Grow canceled the attack on Brest, reversed his columns and by August 10th had destroyed this German threat on the thrust into Brittany.

Web's 50th Arm'd. Inf. Bn. was given the assignment to capture Hill 105 outside of Brest. It looked down on the harbor – a strategic position in the German defense. If the Americans could gain control, their artillery could decimate the city from this vantage point. This was hedgerow country. Hedgerows were heavily foliated banks of soil, sometimes 4-6 feet high separating the small farm fields, usually with a horse-cart path running along the edge. Trees and bushes grew entangled on the bank tops. Many of these Brittany hedges were centuries old. They were great places for defense, but Hell for an attacking force. The Germans were expert in the defense of hedgerows – Americans had to learn on the deadly job! Often the Germans would put two machine guns in the corners of the hedgerow field for crossfire hoping to trap an American rifle squad inside. Each field had an opening where the farmer could enter with his horse and cart. Armor was next to useless in this country- it was Infantry fighting in each field - one field at a time!

Web tells his story about the well defended Hill 105. On August 12th, his 50th Armored Inf. Bn. was given the job of attacking this hill. Web was on the left flank with his rifle squad of 9 men. As Staff Sergeant squad leader of his men, Web gave directions and instructions to them. A tremendous American artillery barrage opened up on the German positions. It was now time for the attack. Web told his men to keep firing their M-1 Garrand semi-automatic rifles into the hedge rows as they moved forward to keep the Germans pinned down. In addition he had two men, one of which was Pfc. George Williams, manning a 30 caliber machine gun on his left flank firing for coverage. Both George and his partner were killed later in the day when German machine guns zeroed in on their position

The first attack on Hill 105 gained about 400 yards in the morning but was repulsed by extremely heavy small arms fire and 20 mm and 40 mm automatic weapons. The 50th AIB and Web's squad were moved back to reorganize for another attack later in the afternoon. Web was short a couple of men in his squad. Web asked his Company Commander, Lt. Newman for some help – replacements. Lt. Newman replied that there were no replacements available – the 6th Armored had dashed 200 miles into the Brittany peninsula toward Brest.

Later that day they were given orders to again attack this steep hill about 500 yards west of their original assault. Web led his squad once again in single file up the hill, spread out, alongside a hedgerow. In Web's own words, " I ordered the guys as we walked up that hill to keep pumping bullets into that hedgerow way over on the side and the front. We moved along pretty good. I was surprised. Boy, those rifles really got hot! When we got near the top of the field, I didn't know how we didn't pin all the Germans down, but somebody got a shot off and hit Pfc. Paul Holon in the eye and out the side of his head – believe it or not! So, the minute he went down, we all hit the ground. I'm up forward heading the squad – the things that go through your mind – I want to get the Hell out of here. You start thinking, you don't go back - you're going to get hurt more going backward than going forward. You learn that! I knew we couldn't stay there long or we'd be sitting ducks. I got the word back to the men, to cover me as I'm going to throw a grenade over the top of the hedge. As soon as I get going, follow me, shooting as you go." He threw his grenade into the German side of the hedge and it exploded.

Web continued, "Just then a German threw a grenade over the hedge at me. Boy, I heard that tell-tale snap (*the sound of a live delayed fuse*) and I tried to outrun it. Well, it went off, knocked me down, blew my helmet off. That's why you don't strap your helmet on under your chin, because if you get a terrific blast it can break your neck! That's something else we learned. I didn't know I was hit in the back by little pieces of shrapnel from that potato masher *(the German hand grenade, so named because of what it looked like to GI's)* .When I gained control of myself, I turned, expecting to see my squad. So, 22 year old Sgt. Dan Seroskie (Asst. Squad Leader) saw me go down, thought I was killed, turned around and went back toward Holon. Dan was my right hand man and a good one! He then took care of Holon , bandaged his eye and head as best he could. I didn't know it at the time, but Dan told me German medics picked up Paul Holon and took pretty good care of him. He became a POW.

It was starting to get dark. There was enough cover in the tall weeds for the remaining squad members to hide or they would all have been picked off. They later crawled down the hill after dark to the American lines.

Web got back on his feet in a minute or so after recovering from the blast of the potato masher, and picked up his helmet. Web went on," I was about to go back for my squad when I looked ahead and saw our Lieutenant, a member of our squad, Joe Hand, and two other soldiers from our platoon. The Lieutenant wanted me to join them on an attack into the next field. I warned him of the danger in the area but the Lt. insisted on moving up the hill through a hedgerow opening. This Lieutenant had been wounded in the South Pacific theater, and then they sent him to Europe as a replacement and he was green. He thought the five of us could gain and hold the next hedgerow before dark... I wasn't in favor of it because we had no back-up fire power! He said, ' Follow me' as he made a dash across an opening for the protection of the hedgerow leading to the top of the hill. The rest of us followed and luckily drew no fire. As we started to creep forward, we received a heavy stream of enemy fire, clipping the hedgerow just above our heads.

It was then that the Lt. decided we would never make it, ordering us to follow him back through the opening. But, this time the German riflemen had the opening zeroed in.

The Lt. dashed first to the opening in the hedgerow and he was hit right in the head - killed! His helmet went flying off. He made a flying dive, right down! We were told by Col. Wall - when we went up the second time... and he knew it was getting late in the day...any ground that you hold on the hilltop, dig in! Those were the orders.!" It's easy to give orders back at headquarters.

Web went on, " I was now in charge of the remaining three. We were pinned down and wouldn't dare peek over the top of the hedgerow... if we didn't get out of this spot, I knew they would get in a position to shoot straight down the line at us and we all would have had it! I asked the other three if they had any grenades and each nodded, 'Yes'. It was impossible to throw a grenade into the enemy position...much too far. I knew if I could get their eyes off their sights long enough, we might get back through that opening. I gave orders for each man to throw a grenade into the field as far as possible, two seconds apart and then run for the opening. We made it!

In the dark Web lost contact with the other three as they moved along a path quietly. He was alone in German territory. Web found a haystack close to a hedgerow one field east of the spot where the Lieutenant was killed. He was exhausted. He used his intuition and crawled on the ground under the haystack feet first. " I wanted to see what was going on out there – if I had to look or get out of there in a hurry", He added, " I was so exhausted by the long day and all of the strain that I just conked out! The battle was still going on – you could see tracers against the darkened sky. I was too tired to dig a hole. I saw that haystack and figured it was a good place to go 'til morning. Unknown to me, orders came for the 50th Armored Infantry Battalion to move off the hill.

So, when I woke up early in the morning, I heard activity and I thought for sure it's our guys. It was time to crawl out to contact Company "A". I thought it odd that I didn't hear any shooting. I was just about to push my way out and I heard the words and voice of a German soldier. I peeked out and saw these hobnail boots walking back and forth. Just then an American artillery barrage came in - close – blew the top off the haystack. The German soldiers all scattered to their foxholes and bunkers. I thought, if I'm ever going to get out of here alive, now is my chance to get through the hedgerow and run down the path." So, he jumped through the branches of the hedgerow bushes on to a path down the hill toward a railroad track. He knew there was a farmhouse near his

21

attack jumping off spot. Web continues, "Once I got down there I thought Oh Boy! I've got it made. What a relief! I thanked the Lord that I was safely off that hill.

When I started going down this narrow path, I heard a low-flying airplane and when I looked up it was a British Spitfire. I heard machine gun fire coming from the field next to me. So, I parted the hedgerow and here are three Germans shooting at this fighter airplane. Now I'm right back in it again! I figured, if there are Germans here they must be all around. Along the path leading to the house, I spotted some heavy foliage-good cover. After making certain no one was in sight, I made a dash for it and crawled into the foliage and settled in.

What went through my mind was, I'll have to stay here 'til after dark and try to crawl out! I checked what I had in my canteen – a little bit of water and I had part of a candy bar. I wouldn't dare light a cigarette. I waited silently. Shortly, I heard some noise. I heard some talking and here were these little kids walking around trying to find things that our guys left behind that they could pick up. There were five kids, ages I guessed from eleven down to five years old. So, I took a chance when the older boy, about 11 years old, came real close. I motioned to him and he crawled right in with me.

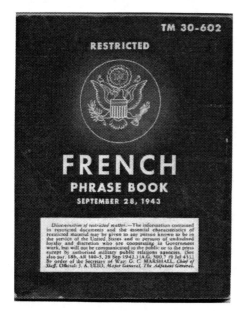

I took out my little English to French book which many GI's carried. The first thing I asked him was where are Les Boches? He looked at me and said, ' Les Boches all around. I go now but I be back'. He called his brothers and sisters together and took off.

I was chewing on part of my chocolate bar when a German officer and two Sergeants came into view – they walked toward the house.

It was quite awhile before the little boy came back. He put his head in the

22

bushes and said, 'You come, come!' I thought, I don't know about this, but what have I got to lose? I picked up my rifle and followed him knowing my safety and my life was in his hands. Remarkably, he had his little brothers and sisters placed all along the path as lookouts. They would signal with their hands, when it was safe for me to go, also when I had to dive back into the foliage - and I had to dive in a hurry! They knew where the Germans were.

I moved from one kid to another until I saw a German soldier talking to one of the little girls. He couldn't have been a guard – maybe he was throwing something out from the mess. He stopped to talk to her. Finally he left. It was amazing to see these little children in action. At their tender age, they seemed to know what they were doing.

The young lad and I reached the woods. He became completely relaxed, threw up his arms and said, 'no more Les Boches - Americans up ahead! Have you cigarette for PaPa?' I gave him everything I had and all my French francs. I asked him where the Americans were and he pointed to the direction saying it was about one kilometer. I showed him my rifle and he walked with me and got me up to the road. Lucky enough, here comes a Jeep with two American soldiers. I hailed them. Now came the time to say goodbye to my little friend. Although he couldn't understand English, I'm sure that he knew the deep thanks owed to him and the other kids. I drove off in the Jeep, turning to wave a last farewell to him and as he disappeared from sight, I realized that I didn't have his name.

Driving to the Company 'A' area, the traumatic events of the experience hit me. I lit up one of the cigarettes the other soldiers gave me and almost went to pieces. You don't realize the mental strain you go through until it's over! They took me back to the command post.

When I reported back to Lt. Newman, he told me, ' I was just ready to report you missing in action! One of our platoon commanders, was killed by our own artillery and he was a good officer! '."

The platoon Medic checked the shrapnel in Web's back from the German hand grenade. Web was peppered with a lot of small pieces, none life threatening, and the

Medic did his best to pick out as many as he could and then put small bandages on the wounds. Web stayed in action with his outfit leading his squad.

During this time in early August, the German high command planned and executed their last large offensive battle in France upon demand by Hitler. The objective was designed to cut the American Third Army of Patton from their supply lines by driving Panzer divisions west to the Atlantic ocean toward Avranches. Patton's two armored divisions were in the Brest peninsula – a great distance from other American Corps.Then Hitler hoped to turn north and chew up the American forces piecemeal. This is known as the battle of the Falaise Gap and many history books have been written about this battle. Hitler's panzers were stopped on this offensive drive by a heroic stand of the American 30th Infantry division at Mortain, after advancing only a few miles. American Generals, Eisenhower, Bradley and Patton saw an opportunity to trap the entire German Army in Normandy – although they differed in strategy.

Patton wanted to race east all the way to the Seine river near Paris and trap the whole German Army. Montgomery and Bradley chose a more conservative approach and since they were Patton's senior in command, their plan was placed into action.
They directed Patton's Third Army east toward LeMans and then north to trap the Germans near Falaise while the British and Canadians crunched down from the north toward Falaise to trap the entire German army in Normandy.

Patton sent his 4th Armored Div., which had been near Rennes, scurrying east. He needed to fill this gap in his lines, so he sent the bulk of the 6th Armored Div. to Rennes. This left Web's 50th AIB along with the 8th Infantry Div. to seal off the port of Brest with it's 20,000-40,000 German troops in defense. The GI's remaining for this job were known as the "Brassiere" boys to hold Brest. Web's sector was thinly held by the Americans. His squad was down to eight men – every squad was short-handed. The Germans didn't know there was such a small force surrounding them. The GI's used many tactics to fool them including driving vehicles back and forth on dusty ground. The clouds of dust indicated massive forces of Americans!

As the days went by after August 12th, German patrols became bolder discovering the wide space between small 50th AIB squads. Night time was especially dangerous. Web tells this story about how seven men of his squad out of eight were captured by the Germans. " There was a farmhouse over here with a trail nearby and of course hedgerows with a little opening. I had a fellow on guard, a new private to the squad. I don't want to mention his name, but Sgt. Seroskie said later, 'If I ever get my hands on him, I'll take care of him! We were dug in our slit-trenches and we covered ourselves with our ponchos to keep the chill and dampness out. The outlook falls asleep. The Germans came through the opening.' Web continued his story, ' Seroskie said that the next thing he knew, a German flipped his poncho off, pointed his rifle at him, told him Hande hoch *(hands up)*. Then they went down the foxhole line and did the same thing with all seven of my guys. Pretty soon they're walking off with all seven of them! About that time this other guy wakes up. He threw a hand grenade and woke everybody else up. I got out of my hole and ran with my rifle to where my guard was and he's yelling his head off! The Germans are coming! I told him to shut up and asked where our squad was. He yelled, they took them, they took them! The slickest patrol, the Germans coming right in and walking off with your men!

Dan Seroskie wrote a letter to Web after the war describing his treatment as a prisoner of war. " All we got to eat for breakfast was a cup of coffee, piece of bread with lard. For dinner you might have got the same thing as you got for breakfast & a piece of meat. Supper you got soup with only potatoes – no vegetables and three cigarettes a day. The Red Cross gave us soap to wash, tooth paste and a few candy bars. We were treated Ok. We used to see the bombers *(American)* bombing Brest… we would sit on the bank across the river from Brest".

So now we have hardly anybody in our squad – just two of us. Capt. Newman comes running over wondering what all the noise is about. I explained what happened. Now Captain, 'can you get me some more men for my area? He answered, 'I don't have any!' I asked him what I'm supposed to do during the next night. He said that you'll have to take care of this whole area. Night came and we were really jittery.

In the meantime, some engineers from Headquarters Company boobie trapped the house nearby so this wouldn't happen again. Anyone tripping the wires would set off the explosion. The sad part of this is the French family came back during the day and set off a boobie trap. We sent our Medics in there to help them out.

They sent up a brand new Lieutenant that was roaming around the area. After dark things were real quiet – there were just two of us in this area. I could hear a sound – like metal hitting against a rock. I listened,- it was like scraping and digging. I called the Lieutenant over and I asked him what he thought about the noise. He said that he thought the Germans were digging in and maybe they were going to hit us in the morning. So, he said, ' here's what we'll do. We'll call back to our 105mm artillery guns and have them put some shells in there'. Gee, it was only a short distance away - maybe 50 -100 yards. I said it's going to be close, isn't it? He called back to artillery, gave them the coordinates while we hunkered deep in our slit-trenches. Next we could hear the boom, boom, boom of the guns firing. Boy, the shells came in screaming over our heads. The artillery pounded that area. When the firing was all over, we listened and could hear moaning coming from the field next to us. Later, all was quiet. We had to put up with this for six days."

The campaign in the Brest peninsula continued with the 35th Infantry division replacing the part of the 6th Armored still in the area. A short time later in August, Web said," I got my seven squad members back. I asked Sgt. Seroskie what happened. He said, 'Well they marched us over to the Crozon peninsula.' Web asked him, How did you make out?" Seroskie replied,' We were treated all right.' I said I know why you were treated that way because the Germans knew they could not hold out very long." Since the Germans were cut off in the Brest peninsula, there was no way to send prisoners back to Germany.

On September 9th, the 50th Armored Infantry Battalion headed east across France to tie into the rest of the 6th Armored Division. The German army in Normandy was finished by late August, suffering an enormous defeat in the Falaise Gap trying to escape through a narrow opening of a few miles near Chambois. 370,000 German soldiers were squeezing thru this area in retreat and were pounded by artillery and Allied low level fighter aircraft. British Spitfires were especially effective with rockets against the slow moving columns. General von Kluge was relieved of his command by Hitler having been implicated in the July 20th assassination attempt on Hitler at his headquarters in East Prussia, Wolfschanze. He wrote a letter to Hitler on the way home to Germany pleading to stop the war. He stepped out of his car and committed suicide by biting into a cyanide pill.

Monty was slow in moving his British and Canadian troops south through Falaise to close the neck of the trap. Gen. Omar Bradley was afraid to send the Americans closer to the British and Canadians for fear the two armies would be shooting at each other. He halted the Americans near Alencon while the Germans escaped.

General Eberbach, without Hitler's permission, realized the precarious position of German forces and got his prime panzer divisions, their Generals and their staff out of the trap first-- beginning August 13th.The ones left behind to be slaughtered were the horse drawn artillery, wagons and soldiers from east European countries that were forced into the German army. 250,000 Germans escaped through the narrow trap and they were the same panzer divisions that came back to haunt the Allies in December in the Battle of the Bulge. They went back to Germany, refitted, brought in new replacements and settled down behind the Siegfried line to protect the Fatherland. The carnage looked like Dantes Inferno to witnesses. It was estimated that 10,000 were killed and 50,000 Germans captured while losing all of their guns, tanks and equipment.

Allied supply lines lengthened each mile they advanced through France, Belgium and Holland in the Fall of 1944 toward the German border. German supply lines shortened and Hitler promised German people that his secret weapons would turn the tide. Those weapons were Buzz Bombs – flying ram-jet bombs - that were aimed at England, V-2 rockets that were launched toward England from the lowland countries falling on London and the first jet fighter aircraft, the Messerschmidt 262 that got into the war in 1945. The Allies ran out of gas and supplies. The war developed into one of attrition after the stunning rout of the Germans from France!

Eisenhower was under pressure to keep the offense moving. He knew that the sooner the war ended, the fewer casualties for soldiers and civilians. The Allies were also afraid German scientists might come up with an atom bomb. The US Army got bogged down fighting a series of battles – Patton's Third Army around the heavily defended Metz area and the 1st Army under General Hodges fighting the Battle of the

Hürtgen Forest near Aachen. Winter was approaching and the Allies were making little progress but suffering huge casualties – mired in a stalemate situation, exactly the kind of war they did not want to fight! In November 1944, German war production hit its peak – in spite of the huge bombing raids against German cities. The Germans were getting ready to make a stand at the Siegfried line.

Hitler had other things in mind. In September, he secretly planned "Wacht am Rhein" the German offensive in the Ardennes. On December 16,1944, 250,000 panzer troops attacked the thinly held American lines in Belgium and Luxembourg catching the Americans completely by surprise. The Battle of the Bulge, as Americans know it, became the largest land battle fought ever fought by the American army.

Many great books have been written by historians about this tremendous battle at the end of 1944 running through January 1945. It was fought under the worst possible weather conditions. It was the coldest, snowiest winter in Europe for decades. Hitler thought he could send his panzers crashing through the thinly held American lines defended largely by new green divisions and replacements. He planned to cross the Meuse river, race on to Antwerp, thereby splitting the American and British armies in two. Then the Whermacht could wipe out both separately - just like the Germans trapped the British on the beaches at Dunkirk in June 1940.

Americans, overwhelmed at first, slowed the German advances beginning from day one. In the center of the attack in Luxembourg, the 28th Infantry Div, commanded by Gen. Coata, who landed on Omaha beach on D-Day with the 29th Inf. Div, held out for three days. They collapsed under the German pressure on December 18[th.]. This division was carved up in the Hürtgen forest battles in November and was largely a division of replacements. The heroic stand of the 110th Inf. Regt. of the 28th Inf. Div. at Clervaux, Luxembourg, out-manned 10-1, delayed the panzers long enough for the 101st Airborne Dv. to get into Bastogne from the Paris area.

On the northern shoulder of the bulge, the 99th and 2nd Inf. Divs. held the Germans from breaking through at Elsenborn, Belgium. The new 106th Inf. Div.was not so lucky. They were surrounded by the Germans in the "Schnee Eifel" and two Regiments of Infantry surrendered – over 7,000 American troops – the largest surrender in US Military history. They became German POW's, living through Hell in German camps. Those who survived, were liberated in April 1945. Among the American troops captured was Kurt Vonnegut, who wrote about this in "Slaughter House Five."

South In Luxembourg, the 4th Infantry Div.and Combat Commands of the 9th Armored Div. held the Germans in check. The first day of the battle, Gen. Omar Bradley thought it was only a spoiling attack. Shortly, Gen. Eisenhower identified it as a major offensive and took immediate steps to counter the attack. He ordered all available trucks to stop what they were doing and haul troops and ammunition to the front! He then sent his only two reserve divisions, the 101st and 82nd Airborne, into battle to reinforce the front. The 101st went to Bastogne arriving late on Dec. 18th along with a Combat Command of the 7th Armored Div. This historic battle has been well recorded by many authors. The Americans were surrounded, out-numbered, battered by enemy artillery and bombing attacks. This town was one of two key crossroads that the Germans needed. Hitler demanded that Bastogne be taken! German officers presented a surrender offer to Gen. Anthony McAuliffe and the American general responded with his famous comment, "Nuts!"

On December 19th, Gen. Patton anticipating that his 3rd Army would be needed in the battle, pivoted his armored divisions in the Metz area 90 degrees and rushed them north toward Bastogne. Both the 4th Armored and the 6th Armored were on the move. On December 26th, units of the 4th Armored reached Bastogne and the encirclement was breached. But, the battle was not over – it went on another month, until the end of January!

Web now found himself in the Battle of the Bulge after fighting in France near Verdun, the largest battle of World War I, through the rain soaked months of October, November and December. Patton was bound to take Ft. Driant, indestructibly fortified, outside of Metz and slugged it out for two months in the mud. The Third Army in November alone lost 23,000 killed, wounded and missing in action and for December the numbers were 53,904. More replacements were needed. In Patton's own words," The situation as to replacements was now extremely bad. In an army of six infantry divisions and three armored divisions we were eleven thousand men short, which, being translated into terms of riflemen – and they are the people who get hurt – meant that the rifle companies were at only fifty-five per cent of their strength." Some historians, including Stephen Ambrose, maintain that the American winter offensives of the Hürtgen Forest and Patton's attacks in the Metz- Nancy area did not shorten the war one day. They just wasted the lives of soldiers in a World War I type stalemate that gained only a few miles of worthless territory in the mud! It was a war of attrition.

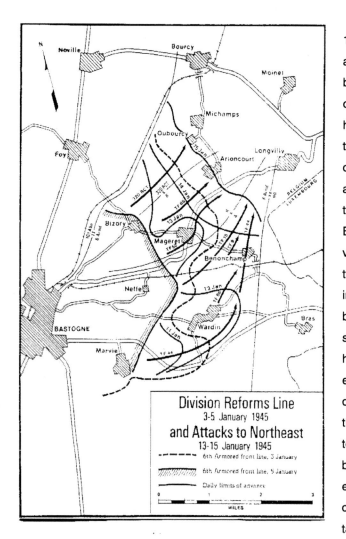

Division Reforms Line
3-5 January 1945
and Attacks to Northeast
13-15 January 1945
- - - - - 6th Armored front line, 3 January
////////// 6th Armored front line, 5 January
――――― Daily limits of advance

0   1   2   3
MILES

On January 1, 1945, Web was dug-in a foxhole along with his buddies just northwest of Bastogne near the hamlet of Bizory, less than two miles from the center of the city. In this area of Belgium and typical of northern Europe, there is a small village or hamlet every two or three kilometers in all directions. Farm buildings are made of stone and brick. They house cattle and equipment, while each day farmers go out of the village into the fields to work. These stone buildings make excellent defensive cover for machine guns, tanks and artillery

Map courtesy of Sixth Arm'd. Assn., George Hoffman's THE SUPER SIXTH 1975

For the next ten days the battle for Bastogne went back and forth with very little territory gained by the Americans or the Germans – in the bitter cold, ice and snow!

The command to attack to the northeast once again was set for January 13th. The 6th Armored Div. and the 50th Armored Inf. Bn. headed toward the village of Mageret, less than 1 mile away, the main road to Luxembourg. By this time, division strength was down to 50 per cent – but, orders to attack came anyway! War doesn't stop for casualties!

What was it like to be a combat infantryman in the Battle of the Bulge in Belgium and Luxembourg in the winter of 1944-1945?

Web Halvorsen tells the story in his own words. "The night before the attack, we were back in the woods and in the neatest German dugout. Boy, those Germans built some almost half the size of a room complete with thick log roofs to protect from artillery shrapnel. We had a candle in it and a new lieutenant came in along with some other soldiers. Officers got a ration of liquor and he had a bottle of whisky which he shared with everyone. About that time, we got some mail. This one gal that I knew, Jewel Bennett from Rogers Park, her folks sent me a cake. Can you imagine… that we got that cake up there in a box? I'll never forget sharing that cake with everyone while we had a nip of that whiskey.

We had to walk toward Mageret. By the time we got there, it was getting dark. I'll tell you, it was at that time in the service with me, going at it from Utah beach to Mageret, I just about had it. My back was killing me! I kept moving my rifle from one shoulder to another. I was dragging along. Being only the 7th guy left in the whole company and all these replacements, I felt I was just starting to get battle fatigue!
I got to thinking what was making my back so sore. I was carrying 4 grenades, a canteen – frozen most of the time, a canteen holder on the other side which I used to hold more grenades, a bayonet, shovel, two bandoliers of M-1 ammunition over my shoulders plus an M-1 rifle *(nine pounds)*. My back was just burning-stinging.

Finally we got in position on a hill above town. We had a new replacement officer sent up to us. He said to me, ' Sergeant, how are you? How long you been with the outfit?' I said since Utah beach. He said, ' Sergeant, you take over!' When we got on top of that little knoll looking down into Mageret, the orders were to get into that town. We had a platoon surrounded down there. Before we got started, we got one or two guys hit not too far from me. This was in the dark (*it gets dark in Europe at this time of year by 4:00 PM*). Capt. Rimmer said, ' Halvorsen, we've got to get down there and lets not waste any time! Get your guys to run it!' This meant run and shoot, run and shoot. So I told the guys to take two shots and move- get down into the town as fast as they could! We moved along that way. Somehow, I got down into a kneeling position to fire thinking that I would be a smaller target. So I made one more move, fired and the damn gun jammed from the cold. In a second I started working on the bolt to get the gun freed. Phsht! It caught me. I was hit! "

It is important to know that Germans had smokeless and flashless gun powder, while American ammunition emitted a puff of smoke and a flash when fired. This was a huge advantage for Germans on the defensive to locate attacking GI's – especially at dusk or night. How many American casualties were caused by this? Web was carrying an Army K-ration box in his upper right hand field jacket pocket. K-ration boxes were about the size of a "Cracker Jack" box. Most often one of the food energy items included was a fruit bar. It was a hard pressed small bar of prunes and raisins. GI's could bite off a chunk to help kill hunger pains. Web said that the bullet went through Army straps, the K-ration box and the hard fruit bar, all his clothing and bones - it must have been enough to stop the bullet from exiting his back.

Web continues, " You are lucky when the bullet does not go all the way through because the hole going out is much larger than the hole going in. You know you're hit in the lung when blood comes out of your mouth. My glasses popped off, but I found them – picked them up. I had this fellow next to me. He said, ' You hit Sarge?' I could hardly talk. I stretched out on my back. He said, ' I'll go and try to get a Medic!' " Web later got a letter from him when he got back to Washington saying, ' I sure remember when you were hit. We had a Helluva time getting you out of there'.

"On that particular attack, I got hold of an Army blanket. I never took a blanket before. I thought I'm going to take this blanket with me. I'll take some rope and just throw it over my back. That could have saved me, too. When I got hit somebody there cut it off my back. If my back couldn't straighten out, I probably would have choked to death with blood coming out of my mouth – it was like vomiting blood!

I prayed everyday and I was brought up with a strong faith. All I could think of, by myself while lying in the snow on my back looking up at the stars in the sky, was in World War I, I knew when you were hit in the chest, you wouldn't make it. If I didn't move, I didn't have any pain. I looked up at the sky and felt at peace with myself. I wasn't worried. If I was going to die I was ready to accept it. I could hear other wounded guys screaming, but I was going to hang on as long as I could!

Finally a Medic came and it's tough because you have all these clothes and equipment on. So, he did his best to unbutton me – took out some sulpha and put it on my chest wound - he thought. In the dark and cold he only got down to my GI long underwear. Put a patch on it. Soon guys with a stretcher came, rolled me into the stretcher and that was really painful. While waiting for the Jeep, they covered me with my blanket, so maybe that helped save me. They put me up onto a two-man stretcher Jeep and drove to an aid station. I got to the aid station, which was some stone house near the front." Plasma came packaged in powder form and had to be dissolved in saline solution. Some medic units got their first batch of penicillin, which also came in powder form, during the Battle of the Bulge. " Dr. Vincent took a look at me and they didn't waste any time. The first thing I said to Dr. Vincent was, how big is the hole in my back? I could hardly talk above a whisper. He said, ' We'll take a look!' They rolled me over. He said, 'You don't have a hole in your back.' Two or three guys went to work on me with scissors – up one pants leg, up the other – up one sleeve and up the other. It's like skinning a rat! Then I went into the meat wagon (*ambulance*) to Bastogne where Major Lamar Soutter operated."

Major Soutter, a famous thoracic surgeon, was 200 miles in the rear near Paris when the Battle of the Bulge broke out, working in a Third Army surgical field hospital. He and his crew were talking about a Christmas dinner when an officer came by asking for medical volunteers to go to Bastogne. The officer said there were 1500 casualties and only one surgeon tending to them. The next day Maj. Soutter, his assistant and anesthetist went to an air strip and climbed into a glider with their medical gear. They were towed by a C-47 plane to Bastogne. They glided to a safe landing within the surrounded American lines after running through a gauntlet of German anti-aircraft fire. He's the one who operated on Web.

Web continues, " After I got out of the meat wagon I was pretty doped up – morphine. They put me on one of those high roller stretchers and I just waited my turn because that's the way it was. It was awhile before I was operated on." His clinical hand written record at the field hospital confirms that Web had to wait his turn for surgery – over fifteen hours. The nurse wrote, "Jan.14,1945 – 11:am - patient returned from surgery to post operating ward under anesthesia. Respiration poor" He had been given two bottles of plasma and three 500 cc units of whole blood. Web's incision scar runs from the front of his chest all the way around to the middle of his back. The upper lobe of his right lung, damaged by the bullet, was removed.

"After the surgery, I woke up in intensive care. Do I ever remember that! I had clean white sheets, there was no pain, and here I had a nurse and she had cleaned me up with a sponge bath. Man, I'll tell you, after being out in the cold in foxholes for months, it was like waking up in a dream! I don't think I stayed in intensive care for more than one full day because they had so many wounded coming in. They moved me out into a ward with the rest of the casualties.

Dr. Soutter came around on morning call and asked me, ' How are you feeling?' I told him everything was fine except for that sting in my back when I move! He said, ' Let's roll you over and take a look'. Then he took his fingers, felt around my lower back and found the bullet just under my skin. He called the nurse over with her little cart. He asked for a scalpel and tweezers. He said to me, ' This might hurt a little bit Sergeant'. He bulged the bullet to the surface with his fingers, took his knife and made a deep cut. He reached in with the tweezers, gave a pull and came out with the bullet holding it up saying, ' Sergeant, here's a souvenir for you!' " Web knew then that the bullet must have entered his chest after going through the K-ration box and the tough pressed fruit bar. This slowed the impact of the bullet enough so it didn't exit through his back.

In a couple of days Web perked up then was transferred back to another field hospital before going on to a general hospital in Paris. " I wasn't there but two days and a nurse came around and said that I was going back to England. German prisoners came into the hospital and carried us out to the ambulances. They took us to the railroad station where the had bunks built into box cars to carry the stretchers. We went to LeHavre, boarded a ship and wound up at a hospital near Plymouth".

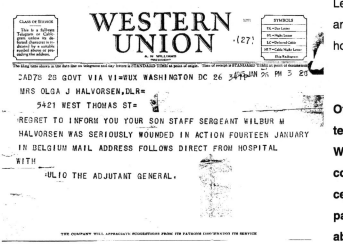

On the 26th Of January, 1945, this telegram was sent to Web's mother. The contents would most certainly cause any parent to deeply worry about their loved one!

By the 5th of February Web was ambulatory. He wrote a letter home:

" Dear Folks,

Well, I am finally settled and now I have an APO number. I will get my mail direct. You will probably be surprised when I tell you that I am now back in England. I was almost sure I would return here. Yes, I can imagine that the thought running through your mind is that I must be a serious case. No, it doesn't necessarily mean that. Most cases are sent back to England so the hospitals in France won't be cluttered up. I saw them building all these hospitals before I went across (to France) last summer. There was one near the Searches and I was sort of hoping I would be sent there, but I am nowhere near there. What gets me is that I can't say where I'm at. However, Edith can find out through the Red Cross after she knows my address. If she's at the same place, we won't be so far apart. She could either come here or I could go to her in an afternoons' time.

I was wondering if you have received a notification from the government, yet. I can't understand why we can't say anything about our wound, but they claim the censor won't pass it. I guess they figure they could tell you more about it than I can. I guess there isn't much to say about it anyway. All I can say is I sure have been lucky. When I look about me and see some of the cases I have seen, I can thank God how fortunate I have been. I have my arms & legs, I haven't been disfigured in any way and I have all my senses which means everything in the world. After a man goes so far in this war he isn't a bit surprised when he gets hit and that is just the way I felt about it.

I believe I am now safe to tell you that it was in the Bastogne area that I saw my last bit of action. I am sure you have read a great deal about the fighting in and around that, now, well known city. It was quite a nip and tuck battle for a few days until we pushed the Jerries back. It was there we were entering a town one night when the Heinies opened up with a machine gun. We opened fire and shut it up for awhile and then it started again. I fired a few shots and then my gun jammed. Like a fool I stayed in the same spot trying to get my rifle working and naturally the Jerries picked up my flash and opened up and I caught one slug. I was lucky I didn't catch a half a dozen of them. Later one of the men slipped up and dropped a grenade directly in the middle of them and finished the whole lot of them.

Not long after I was taken care of by one of the best doctors in the ETO. It got me sort of mad to think of one of those Huns getting a shot at me. If it would have been daylight it would have been different. I could always hold my own then and did for six months. We didn't do much fighting at night and that is where I slipped up.

Now the Russians and our troops are pushing and crushing the enemy on all sides. It looks bad for Hitler and his gang and it looks like he is going to get it good this time.

This seems to be a very good hospital. The food is good. All day long we have good music. And this afternoon we enjoyed a good movie. I have been in a lot of hospitals and I can say they are all very good.

While I was in Paris I couldn't manage to get the perfume but I have the address of a fellow there and he is going to send me some, so I haven't given up hope.

You can address my letters as following-
U.S. Hospital Plant 4101
A.P.O. 168 c/o Postmaster
New York, New York

One thing that I need now that I wash and shave every day & that is some hair stay. It is almost impossible to get any here.

It is almost time for the lights to go out so I better close.

With all my love,   Web

By the time Web got to England, he could get up and walk around which the medics encouraged. He continued to recuperate – which in itself was a miracle considering the severity of his chest wound. One day he was called into his doctor's office. Web recalls the doctor said, ' You know Sergeant, I have bad news for you. You're not going back to your outfit!' Anybody who lived out in that snow, cold and misery would be off his rocker - crazy to want to go back. 'You'll be leaving here in a few days to be going back to the United States. Whatever you have to pack be ready.'

We boarded a train to Grenoc, Scotland where the Queen Elizabeth was waiting in the sea because she was too big for the dock. On March 11th we went out to the ship, were assigned cabins and by March 17th we passed the Statue of Liberty in New York harbor. (*In the early winter months of 1945, it was much safer to have these huge ships sail full speed ahead at about thirty knots to avoid any possible U-boat attack).* There was one incident that annoys me to this day. Aboard the Queen, we could buy things to take home to your family - chocolates, cigarettes, cigars, perfumes and gifts for my mother and sister. I packed them down in my duffle bag. When we got to New York, we didn't have to carry our bags – German POW's were there to carry them. They told us not to worry about our duffle bags – when you get to your hospital ward, your bags will be waiting for you. Well, when I got to my ward and my bag – you know what happened?

Everything I bought was gone! I never knew whether it was the German prisoners that did the stealing or the MP's guarding the area.

At the hospital in New York we were allowed one phone call home. The mail was so slow, my mother and father didn't know what really happened to me. My mother came to the phone. I said, do you know who this is? She said no. I said it's your son. She said someone must be fooling me! She couldn't believe it was me! Up to that time all the folks knew was the information on the telegram. We had a wonderful visit and I told them what happened. " His phone call home from New York beat the Army mail to his home sent from England.

" I was transferred in a few days to Kennedy General hospital in Memphis, Tennessee. I stayed there quite awhile, in fact I went home on pass for Easter. That's where I got the sad news that my best buddy, Wes Stark, an officer in the Navy had been killed in the Pacific. From Kennedy General I was sent to Percy Jones hospital in Battle Creek, Michigan for rehabilitation and there they had German prisoners which was the safest place in the world for them to be! From there, I was discharged from adjacent Ft. Custer on July 10th, 1945 with 40% disability."

After his arrival back in Chicago, Web thought he'd take it easy for a time to continue his healing process. He wanted to go to Lake Geneva, Wisconsin for the summer. His local doctor advised him to think about going to a warmer climate. He was afraid that in cold weather winter, Web might be more susceptible to flu or pneumonia. By late July, he had a chance to drive to California with his friend, Frank Goyette, in a 1941 Buick convertible. So, after thinking about his doctors advice, he made up his mind to live in a warmer climate. In Glendale, California he stayed with friends, the Dr. Gist family, rooming with their son Don. This was the era for dreaded polio epidemics and his friend Don came down with a 102 degree temperature. He was diagnosed with polio- which affected his walking for the rest of his life.

Web managed to get back to Chicago by train for Christmas to be with his family. He returned to Glendale after a short visit home. He had several small jobs including one at an appliance store. In 1946 he met Leonie Derro while at a dance at the "Wagon Wheel." – where popular orchestras played big band swing music of the Forties. It is ironic that her father was born and raised in the Belgium city, Liege, which is not far from the Bastogne area where Web was wounded. They fell in love and were married in 1947. Leonie had been manager of a bakery that made cookies – many for the military services during the war years. Things improved for Web. He got a job offer from the North Hollywood Mfg. Co. as a sales representative for the Pacific Northwest region. Web and Leonie moved to Seattle where he sold decorative copper and brass accessories as well as artificial flowers to department stores. Since he worked on a commission basis, he did well financially. Web retired in1986. They had a wonderful life together until June 12, 1989 when Leonie passed away after a lung disease.

Web's brother, Don, and his wife Peggy happened to be vacationing in Door county Wisconsin. Peggy went into a very nice tapestry and quilt shop to purchase something for their home. She gave her credit card to the owner of the shop who, of course, read the name Halvorsen. She asked Peggy if by chance she knew of a Web Halvorsen from the Austin area of Chicago. Peggy answered – 'that's my brother-in-law'. It so happened that the owner of the shop who made the inquiry, was Marion Kolb, Web's teenage sweetheart from the Lake Geneva, Wisconsin area. Web had carried her photo in his wallet during the war but they lost track of each other after Web went to California. Here is another Hollywood story! Marion was a widow whose husband had died in 1984. Web made a trip to Door county and their romance renewed itself some 45 years later. They married in August 1990 and now live happily together in Seattle during the summer and they have a winter home in Whispering Pines, North Carolina. What could be a better storybook ending for another World War II hero?

Web and Marion Halvorsen at their winter home in Rockport, Texas in the Spring of 2000

FRANK DYER CIPPERLY

The Cipperly family has lived and farmed in the up-state New York area since the early 1800's. Both Frank's mother and father were born in the USA.. His great-grandfather came to the United States from either Germany or Holland - there are no records. His mother is of English heritage. These hardy rugged folks farmed in the Hoosick Falls area, about twenty-five miles east of the capitol, Albany, and tucked in against the Vermont border near the historical town of Bennington.

They are proud of their local heritage and history – this area is just east of the Hudson River and before the Vermont Green Mountains. They are especially proud of the town of Hoosick (*population 3,490*) where famous artist Grandma Moses grew up. She was a good friend of Mary Wells (*Frank's future wife*) and her family. Harry Edward Cipperly (*1883-1950*) and Alice Webster Cipperly(*1890-1980*) raised their large family on their Hoosick Falls township farm. This hilly area, farmed for decades by early American settlers, is not an easy place to farm. They had to make do with worked over soil, rocks and forests. They had fifteen children and Frank was born August 29, 1918 - right in the middle with seven siblings older and seven brothers and sisters younger. To this day, many Cipperly's stayed in the area, farmed, live close to each other and are employed near Hoosick Falls. When I stopped at a nursery and flower shop for directions to ask if they might know the Cipperly family, the lady responded, " Do I know them! They're all over the place!"

Frank with 13 of his brothers and sisters on June 13,1941 before he went into the Army. He is in the middle of the back row.

Frank tells the story of how Hoosick Falls got that name. Back in colonial times at the local river bank, " Hoosic river got the name of Hoosic 'cuz one man was across the river and hollered back, ' Who's sick?' so the town got the name of Hoosick Falls while the river is spelled without the 'k'. Clarence Sanning, my Company B First Sergeant who I hadn't seen since 1944, remembered that story 55 years later at our final 6th Armored Division reunion – September 2000 in Louisville, Kentucky!"

Frank has fond memories of his childhood on the farm. "We walked to our one room schoolhouse about ¾ of a mile away from the farm- walked home for dinner (*lunch now*) and back to school for the afternoon." All the kids had chores to do, so they grew up knowing what work was about on a farm. He attended Hoosick Falls high school for three years until 1936, when he came down with a case of impetigo during Easter vacation. In those days there was no easy cure for this contagious skin disease. " When I went back to school, they wouldn't let me into my classroom. So, I stayed home another week or two. Well, I went back one day, turned my books in and went home. Spring work started and I always drove the horses so I went to work on the farm. We had two teams of horses – a slow team and a fast team. I drove the fast team. We had one tractor - in 1928 my father bought his first tractor, a Fordson with steel wheels and lugs on it. "

Of course, during the Great Depression years of the 1930's – work on the family farm was not a bad job. You had shelter, plenty to eat and a family to be with. You couldn't make any money since farmers barely made enough from crops to buy seed for the next years' plantings. Frank said, "I know my father, many times, when he had a note come due, he'd go to a neighbor, borrow $50 to pay the note that he owed. When he had to buy machinery, he'd sign a note because he didn't have the cash to pay for it."

"In 1939, I went to work for the county. The highway superintendent came up to my father and wanted to know if one of his boys might want to work for the county. Father asked me if I wanted the job – we really didn't need all of the boys on the farm – so I went to work for the county during the next three summers. I worked on a blacktop machine paving roads. We got paid a dollar an hour."

" In March of 1941 my brother, William, was drafted – he was already in the Army on Pearl Harbor Day, December 7, 1941." Frank was drafted April 10, 1942. The local

draft board took two of the boys and left four at home to help farm. The oldest son, born in 1909, worked for a machinery dealer. The youngest of the seven boys, Robert, was born in 1930 so he was too young for military service then.

" We went to Albany and from there to Camp Upton for three days – then right to Camp Chaffee near Ft. Smith, Arkansas. If you walk across the river bridge in Ft. Smith, you're in Oklahoma. I was immediately assigned to Company H , 50th Armored Infantry Regiment, 6th Armored Division which had been organized earlier in 1942 at Ft. Knox, Kentucky and moved to Camp Chaffee in March." The United States was busy mobilizing armed forces for the battles to come - largely through the draft system.

The division trained there for a year, participating in the Louisiana maneuvers, with obsolete vehicles and tanks. Some divisions wrapped trucks with cardboard and painted "TANK" on the outside for the maneuvers. October 1942, the 6th Armored moved to the Mojave Desert in Southern California for five months of desert training – a real test of machinery in the sand and dust and tough training for the infantry! In March of 1943,

the division found a new home in Camp Cooke, California just north of Santa Barbara.

In July of 1943, Frank got a two week furlough.

" I came home to Hoosick Falls. Oh yes, I met Mary Wells back in 1938 at a card party in nearby Petersburg. We went together for over five years. We decided to get married before I got home – through letters, of course. And, she told everybody that the day I got home, we would be married the next day. On Thursday evening, July 8th we were married in Petersburg! The church was packed and we had Ginger Ale and Fig Newtons. We had limited time on furlough and limited gas for the car.

We spent the first night in Albany and then came back to our home town. The second night of our marriage we stayed with my family and the boys all slept in one room and the girls all slept in a separate room! Mary slept with the girls and I slept with the boys on our second night 'cuz they didn't have no more beds! We took the train to Chicago where we stayed for three days at the Hotel Hamilton. I went on to Camp Cooke and Mary returned home." In World War II, almost all civilian travel was by rail since gasoline was rationed and car owners received an "A" stamp good for only three gallons per week. " Mary had a room in Troy, NY where she went to work for Montgomery Ward."

The 6th Armored Division was preparing for mechanized warfare in Europe at Camp Cooke – plenty of target practice with all the weapons of an armored division. The drudgery of military life in the USA was about to change for the 1944-1945 battle in Europe.

In January,1944, the 6th Armored moved to Camp Shanks, New York, along the Hudson River for embarkation to England. " We were only there one or two days. They give everybody a 24-hour pass to New York City, but I asked them if I could go home. That's all it was, a 24-hour pass. I was only home 6 hours. There was another fellow from Albany and we took the train up – it took us four hours to go up from Grand Central station and four hours to go back to the city. We had to get a taxi from Shanks to New York. My sister drove to Albany to pick me up. Mary and I went to Petersburg and Hoosick Falls so we got to see all our family."

On February 11,1944, the entire 50th Armored Infantry Battalion (about 1000 men) boarded the USS Henrico. They were piped up by an Army band as were most troops at embarkation ports. The ship joined a huge convoy out of New York harbor, past the Statue of Liberty, to make its' way to England and war. Many of those young soldiers would never return home or see their loved ones again.

" The second or third day out, most everybody was sick and I was too. I went to the doctor and he says, ' Too bad, we're all sick!' He thought I was just sea sick. So the next day, I was <u>sick!</u> They took me down to sick bay and diagnosed me with scarlet fever. Yes, I was quarantined and only the doctor came into the room. As soon as we landed in Grenoc, Scotland (*February 25th*), they took me right off on a stretcher and put me in the hospital. Lt. Johnson was standing up on a platform as they was putting me in a small boat and he says,' You are a sorry looking sight ' 'cuz I hadn't shaved for them whole 14 days or whatever it was." Then Frank gives a hearty laugh telling about his misery! " My fingernails was gone, my toenails was gone. They got me across the bay to the other side, raised me up and shoved me right into an ambulance. We went to a Glasgow hospital." Frank was there for more than a month. Since he was a Staff Sergeant (*three stripes above and one below*) by now, they put him in charge of six or seven soldiers who were in the hospital at the same time to make their trip to Burford by train. April 6th, Frank rejoined his outfit in Burford, England in the Cotswolds.

Frank in front of the pig pens at Burford in 1996

In March, while Frank was recovering in the hospital, the 6th Armored Division became a part of Patton's Third Army. Major General Robert W. Grow, commanding General of the 6th Armored was a cavalry man like Patton and the 6th Armored and the 4th Armored became. Patton's favorites – usually getting the most difficult battle assignments. Frank's outfit, Company B, 50th Armored Infantry Battalion, was billeted just outside Burford which is about 65 miles west of London. " We were in pig pens."

" There was three pig pens for Company B. Company A was up on top of the hill at a golf course. There was a crossroads up at the top, one went to Cheltenham and the other went to Oxford. Burford was a small town – only one main street. They raised their pigs in these farm buildings. When it was time to go back to the billets, the Yanks would say – let's go back to the pig pens where we had bunks!" The Company had tent latrines for the soldiers near the pig pens. The American soldiers in England were preparing for the invasion of Europe and they made do with whatever shelter they could find. And, the English people were there to support them!

When asked if he got to meet some nice British folks, Frank said, " I didn't see many girls like some of the others. There was one fella, he went every night and every Sunday to see a girl. She lived on the main street down in a basement. I went with him once one Sunday. We went to church and walked around town and that was the Sunday before we left. The night before we left Burford, we went to the USO show, Olson and Johnson's "Hellzappopin". Frank gives a hearty laugh.

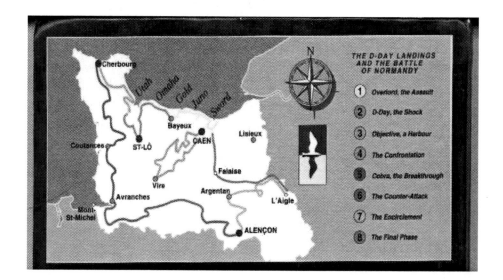

June 6th, D-Day arrived and the soldiers knew something was going on but only learned about it later when the British people heard Gen. Eisenhowers' message on the radio. " We knew something was up, 'cuz the planes kept going. Fifty planes in a group and one group right after another and then they come back."

The 6th Armored's turn to join the battle came in July 1944. Landing on Utah beach between July 18 – 24, when the full division of 10,000 men was battle ready. " Going across the channel, there's another thing. When we were going across the channel, it was so foggy, our boat collided with another boat - we knew we hit something! The next morning when we went down to the half-tracks on board, there was a great big slit in the side of the ship. It was a good thing it was near the ceiling of that deck or we would have sunk in the channel . We had to stay on deck all night."

" The debris on Utah beach was strung all over. We could see the German gun emplacements which had been knocked out and we didn't have any German plane attack us during the landing." Goering's Luftwaffe was not effective during the invasion, Operation Overlord, and the Normandy campaign.

Just what were Frank's duties as a soldier? He was a Staff Sergeant in charge of a 60-mm. mortar squad. At the beginning of the European offensive, each platoon of Armored Infantry had two rifle squads (*12 men each*), one machine gun squad (*12 men*) and one mortar squad (*12 men*). Each platoon had about 50 soldiers led by a 2nd Lieutenant, called a "shavetail" by soldiers. So Frank, being such a modest man didn't say much about why he became a leader. But, he obviously had the proficiency required to handle a mortar squad. Back at Camp Cooke he was promoted to buck Sergeant and then to Staff Sergeant.

What is a 60-millimeter mortar weapon? It is a small stationary cannon that is generally operated by a crew of three men. It looks like a hollow tube mounted on a base-plate which points skyward at an angle. A mortar-man slides the mortar shell into the tube, being very careful to stroke his hand down around the barrel, quickly moving his hand toward the base-plate – making certain no portion of his body is in the way of the trajectory. The finned shell is sent skyward on its' arc as the bottom of the shell hits a stationary firing pin. A 60-millimeter shell is approximately 2 and ½ inches in diameter and detonates as it hits any object usually between 100-1000 yards away. It carries a wallop and is feared by infantrymen. You can hear the "whump" sound when a mortar is fired and then one can count to at least ten seconds before it silently arrives – exploding deadly shrapnel. Some mortar squads became very proficient hitting targets by adjusting the sights or arc. Frank was a good leader of his mortar squad.

" I stood guard every night, just like the rest of them. We all took turns. I kept a sheet in a tablet, one soldier had the first two hours, the next man had the next two hours, etc. I took my turn at two hours just as regular as them. And, we changed every night. If you had first turn tonight, tomorrow you had the second. We rotated positions, too."

On July 15th, German Field Marshall Irwin Rommel wrote, " ...the unequal battle was approaching it's end..." trying to point out to Hitler that it was time to capitulate. For many soldiers, it was just beginning.

The 6th Armored Division was now positioned for action in the VIII Corps, commanded by General Middleton. The 6th was on the extreme right flank of the Allies pushing south through the German lines. On July 25th, the major offensive (*Cobra*) began under the direction of British Gen. Bernard Law Montgomery, "Monty". He called for massive saturation bombing of the German lines south of St. Lo to break the will of the German Panzer Lehr Division fighting in that sector. Over a thousand British and American bombers participated including high level planes (*Strategic Air Force*) and low level bombers (*Tactical Air Force*). This bombing did not accomplish the task without heartbreak for the Allies. The planes were supposed to fly on a west to east line, parallel to the front, but the Air Chiefs of Staff overruled Gen. Omar Bradley's understanding of the bombing plan. The Air Chiefs thought the aircraft loss would be too great from German antiaircraft fire flying parallel to the front. They flew a pattern of approach from north to south.

The sky was partly cloudy. The first waves of planes hit the German lines with tremendous damage. The wind picked up from south to north, blowing into the American lines. Dust from the bombs rose into the sky. Clouds rolled in from the Atlantic ocean. Successive waves of aircraft dropped their deadly load of bombs closer and closer to the American lines and finally onto positions of the 29th and 30th Infantry Divisions. The casualties were more than 400 American soldiers killed!

The Allies knew that the German communication center for the entire Normandy front was located in the St. Lo post office in an underground bunker. The Air Force sent 120 B-26 bombers on a mission to fly a low level attack on this target. They wiped it out and that is the reason the Wehrmacht had so much trouble communicating between command posts. The next day American bombers hit St. Lo again – they destroyed the bridges over the Vire river and the town. 800 civilians were killed in the bombing. They had been warned to leave the area by leaflets dropped from airplanes. The French who survived this bombing hid in the hospital which had 800 beds. It was carved into the side of the rock cliffs near the Vire river.

Because American air power dominated the skies, German troops and supplies could only move toward the front at night. They didn't allow the fleeing French to clutter the narrow roads with their horse carts. Today, in the St. Lo village square, part of the prison façade remains as a monument to the 89 prisoners who were killed in the bombing. The Germans wouldn't release them – almost all were French political officials. Not only soldiers died in the battle of Normandy, but also 10,000 French civilians.

On the 27th of July, the 6th Armored was sent through the lines of the 79th Infantry Division in the breakout of American forces, which had been hemmed in a small area of France for 50 days. Once the Armored Divisions broke through the German lines (*four Armored divisions were on the continent at this time*), their job was to drive fast toward objectives behind German lines, cutting off supplies and creating havoc.

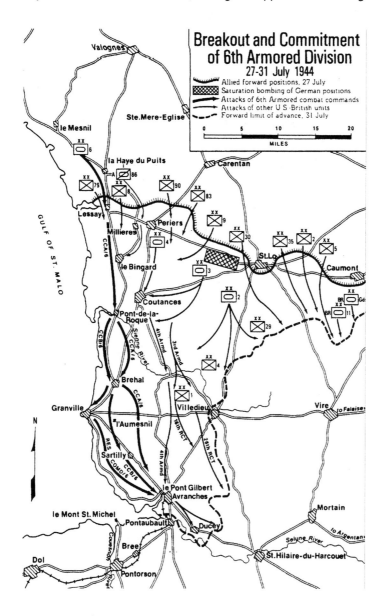

Map courtesy of 6th Arm'd. Div. Assn. George Hoffman's, THE SUPER SIXTH 1975

49

This was Patton's philosophy – move fast, bypass areas of resistance, don't let the enemy have time to set up a defensive position and you will have fewer casualties. The soldiers knew him as "Old Blood and Guts" – our blood and his guts!

Frank tells about the first few days of combat – which soldiers knew as organized chaos! " The first day we headed through Lessay straight down toward Avranches. The next morning we headed south. The first man we lost was Frances Adams that day. He and another guy were killed. Then they sent a rifle squad into the woods off the road to clean up and protect the armored columns and the whole squad was killed. That was our second day."

On July 30th, the 50th Arm'd. Inf. Bn. was advancing toward the small town of Brehal. " We went around the corner in this village and there was a tank sitting there. They stopped us and called in air support. They strafed the other end of the town. When we got to the other end of the town along the road, there were four 88's knocked out that had been pulled by horses. The dead Germans lying in the ditches were their artillery squads. The horses, they stole them from that French village and of course they were killed ,too.

That night we went beyond Brehal, and bivouacked in the hedgerow fields. Someone come back and told me that the tank we saw was from our own 86th Recon (*86th Cavalry Reconnaissance Squadron*) – knocked out and one of my soldier friends that I went in the Army with from Hoosick Falls was killed – Frank O'Neil - it was his tank. He used to go with my sister before he went in the Army."

German Gen. Von Kluge said, " …if the Americans get through Avranches, they can do what they want!" Franks' Company B moved along the same route that Web Halvorsen traveled - through Avranches and into the Brittany peninsula on the way to Brest – some 200 miles west into German territory on a typical Patton dash! In early August, Patton had the 6th Arm'd. in action sealing off Brest and the 4th Arm'd. near Lorient, another port on the Atlantic ocean. He didn't like this strategy – keeping Armored divisions in a static containing position.

Hitler in the meantime had launched his powerful attack on Mortain. The plan was to cut off Patton in the Brest peninsula and then march north and destroy the other American Corps piecemeal. It was a disaster for the Germans. Patton immediately saw the opportunity to trap the entire Normandy Wehrmacht - encircling them by racing toward the Seine River via LeMans. On August 15th with General Omar Bradley's approval, he left the 50th Arm'd. Inf. Bn. and attached artillery units along with a Bn. of the 8th Inf. Div. to hold the Brest front by themselves. The majority of the 6th Arm'd. hurried southeast toward Lorient and relieved the other Arm'd. Division (*the 4th*) in Patton's Third Army. In retrospect, military historians believe the high command of the Allies overestimated the strength of the Germans after the breakthrough. Patton's aggressive use of mobile Armored Divisions could have trapped the entire German army in France, thereby shortening the war. Web told his story of hill 105 and now Frank tells about hill 63 in the Brest encirclement.

"They got in that book, hill 62 , but it was hill 63!. We heard all about the men Company A lost on hill 105. The next day toward evening we went after hill 63. It must have been four or five o'clock and we were going up this road. Lt. Robert Hudson was our platoon leader. We come to a big barn and there was a crossroad and we were assembled in a group right there in the road. They must have decided what they were going to do. We saw a man run. Finally, Lt. Hudson said, 'Lets go, lets go everybody! Everybody lets go!" If that German had got to his machine gun, he could have killed every one of us! But, we all got up the hill together. I don't know how I got ahead. I was the first one up there. When the Germans started throwing grenades - I threw my two grenades. When I looked around there wasn't a soul in site – everybody was in the ditch. I was lucky because only one or two of the German grenades, potato mashers, went off. Thomas, the first man behind me, was a good friend of mine. He was in the machine gun squad. So I took his two and I threw them out. We went back toward the barn and set up our mortar. It was only 100-150 yards to where we fired our shells. Our Sgt., Herman Johnson, he was a nice guy – a little guy. He said that Lt. Hudson went back to the barn to read the maps - but how could you read the maps in the dark? Another time, there was a big ravine. The Lt. wanted him to take us on through that draw. Sgt. Johnson said, ' No, I'm not going down through there'! That's why I liked him.

After we fired our mortar, they called in the artillery. They fired quite a few shots and it was just about dark and here comes 15-18 fellows down the road with their hands up and white flags. They came to where we were. Our men searched them. One Corporal took all of the money, their watches whatever they had! I didn't take nothin' from any of them. I couldn't see that after they surrendered. But, they stripped them of everything they had.

There was a small house on the corner and a Frenchman that wouldn't come down. We lost one man from the 2nd platoon – it was his own fault. His name was Joseph S. Gnot – a tall guy going along a hedgerow. He was walking standing straight up and we hollered at him – **get down, get down**!. Well, he didn't pay no attention and was shot right through the neck just walking through there! That was the only man we lost on hill 63."

Frank remembers the 28th of August. " That was the day the 50th Arm'd. Inf. Bn. was relieved from Brest. The next day, the 29th of August, was my birthday. We walked all day long carrying everything! We hadn't seen our half-tracks for four or five days. Come morning half of us was laying in the road. It was cold! The macadam carried some heat from the sun. The next night we all took a bath, I don't know how many days it had been. This was in a bay - a salt-water bath!

The hedgerows – they were scary! You would be on one side and the Germans would be on the other side – especially at night. On guard every little sound you hear, you wonder. They kept telling you not to look through the hedgerow. I was looking through one and a bullet was so close I felt the heat on my shoulder. That was the closest I came to getting shot then."

" When we left the Brest – Lorient area, we drove straight through towards Nancy. By the 14th of September we were near Troyes, France. We stopped here for three or four days. We played ball and relaxed. We had a big warehouse and Marlene Dietrich put on a USO show one night and it was a good one. From there we went on to Nancy. We regrouped, repaired and got our ammunition supply at the big chateau where we stayed. For three weekends in a row we went out to retake the same town (*Jallaucourt*) from the Germans. I remember one big flat field where the Germans had bunkers – big bunkers! One Sunday when we got there they started shelling us with 88's from the woods to our left. This Lt. Hudson, he jumped in one fellows' foxhole and the guy come and just jumped in right on top of him! After we'd take the town, we'd withdraw and then the Germans would come back in and retake it. Sometimes we got into their bunkers."

That action took place in the Gremecey Forest area just north of Nancy when the rainy weather in fall turned roads into muddy quagmire. *"The Combat History of the Super Sixth"* describes the problem, " Two medium tanks hit mines on the road….and four medium tanks mired down at the edge of town. All six tanks had to be abandoned when the infantry withdrew. These tanks were later destroyed by the enemy." The rain poured down all through the last of September and the month of October. This area is about 20 miles from the German border and resistance stiffened while American supply lines lengthened and gasoline was in short supply. The war was quickly beginning to develop into one of attrition; exactly what SHAEF(*Supreme Headquarters Allied Expeditionary Force*) headquarters did not want to happen.

" We were bivouacked in one cow pasture for more than a week. I had diarrhea and one day, I couldn't even get out of the tent. A lot of us were sick! Our half-track driver was William Crandall who came from Berlin, New York only 10-12 miles from Hoosick Falls. I didn't know him before the Army. We went in the Army at the same time and became friends. He had a son born February 17,1944 while he was on the boat over to Europe - a lot of us from this area wound up in the 6th Armored maybe 60 - 70 or more."

The 6th Armored in October pushed north through the wooded hilly country of the Alsace-Lorraine region. This border area had been fought over by the French and the Germans for ages including the Franco-Prussian war of 1872, World War I in 1918 and now again in 1944.The first action was in Gremecey Forest on October 1st and then the Seille valley attack a week later. The firepower of an Armored division pushed the Germans closer to the Fatherland. But, casualties were high. The terrain favored the defensive positions. According to the written history of the *50th Armored Infantry Bn.*," the balance of October was one of complete rest and relaxation. These troops had fought hard and now they played hard. The nearby city of Nancy, France at once became an amusement mecca, and with passes freely distributed, the men flocked to that famed center of French culture....equipment was repaired and overhauled and weapons were cleaned and cared for."

" President Eisenhower in his 1969 book, "In Review" writes in 1969 ..."The fall period was to become a memorable one because of a series of bitterly contested battles, usually conducted under the most trying conditions of weather and terrain. Walcheran Island, Aachen, the Hürtgen Forest, the Roer Dams, the Saar Basin and the Vosages Mountains were all to give their names during the fall months to battles that, in the sum of their results hastened the end of the war in Europe. Each was of a size to compare with the largest of our Civil War battles or to Waterloo in the Napoleanic wars. In addition to the handicap of weather there was the difficulty of shortages in ammunition and supplies."

By late November the new Mutterbach River offensive took place within 8 miles of the border town, Sarrguemines. This battleground was in the midst of the Maginot line, built in the 1930's by the French as an elaborate impregnable defensive line to keep out Hitler's Nazi Third Reich. It was named after Andre Maginot who served in 26 French Cabinets. The French decided they had to build a fortress defense after the first World War to keep out the Germans. This massive underground series of fortresses was constructed from the Swiss border to the Belgian border near Neufchateau. They did not extend the defenses past their friends – the Belgians. Work began in 1929 and was finished in 1935. Distances between forts ranged from one-quarter mile to one and one-quarter miles. In some places the forts were a complete underground five story city. By May 1938 the Maginot line was fully garrisoned with French soldiers – at the same time of the Anschluss of Austria by Hitler. Naturally, in 1940 when the Wehrmacht took an end run around through the Ardennes in Belgium and got behind the Maginot line, it was a worthless piece of construction – the guns pointed east toward Germany, but the German army had reached the Atlantic Ocean – far to the west behind the Maginot line. Now in 1944, Americans were fighting Germans who had taken over some of the defensive forts in the Maginot line – Frank Cipperly being one of them.

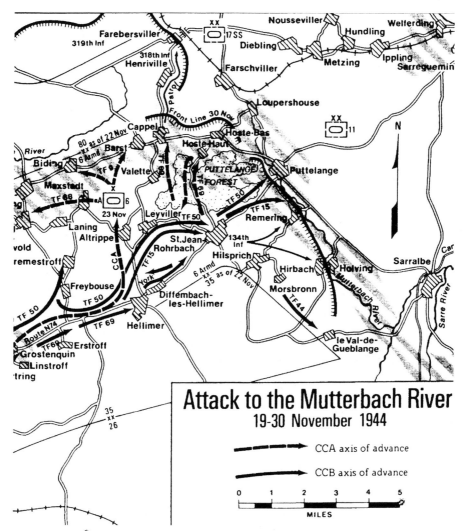

Attack to the Mutterbach River
19-30 November 1944

CCA axis of advance

CCB axis of advance

0 1 2 3 4 5
MILES

Map courtesy of 6th Arm'd. Div. Assn., George Hoffman's, THE SUPER SIXTH, 1975

The attack began on November 19th and by the 22nd the 6th Armored had driven north almost ten miles. Frank's Company B in the 50th AIB had cleared out the town of St. Jean Rohrbach by 3:45 PM – just when it was dusk at this time of year, November 22,1944. " We pulled back into this town to bivouac for the night. There was a Frenchman in the one house we wanted for our squad bivouac and he wouldn't leave his home – he just wouldn't go down there. So, I took him down to Company B headquarters to First Sergeant Clarence Sanning – maybe 150 - 200 yards back from our squad. I just got back to the door of the house, when the shell hit. Bill Crandall, who was in the house with the rest of the squad, told me it was a good thing I had my helmet on 'cuz there was a great big hole in the helmet! They just went out to get me when another shell hit – in almost the same spot! After the first shell, I didn't know nothin'! The Germans had that house and street zeroed in."

From the time the first shell hit, Frank remembers nothing. When asked, who pulled you into the house? – he answered, " Bashford claims he did, Crandall said he was there. Bashford says Crandall was nowheres' near around but he had to be. The medics was right there. The last time Bashford saw me I was placed in the back end of a jeep on a stretcher and it took off. Broward Bashford, Bill Crandall and the other squad members who saw me loaded on that stretcher thought I would never make it. I was hit by both shells 'cuz I was hit all over!

I don't remember anything about the Aid station. I don't know nothin'! If she (*Mary*) could find that letter – I know the nurse come in and wrote the letter – the first letter they got at home. I do remember the 11th of December. The ward boy *(male nurses were called this by the soldiers)*, Pete, came in, he said, ' They said you're going to live and they're going to take you down to get a skin graft on your arm tomorrow'. I'm sure I come to before that. I remember the doctor coming in, a Major at the 100th General Hospital in Bar-le-Duc, France – that was where they took us." Nineteen days passed before Frank regained consciousness! Somehow Frank recalled that the skin graft was the worst pain he suffered – he thought a dull knife was used. He told Pete he would write to him, but, Pete said that's what they all say! Frank felt bad that he couldn't remember Petersons' first name and wished he could have contacted him and the other ward boy, Burt Crawford. Can you imagine how many wounded soldiers went through that hospital in December 1944 – during the Battle of the Bulge?

Mary Cipperly received a telegram from the War Dept. on December 6th saying he was seriously wounded on November 22nd. It didn't give any details about his injuries.

"I know, Christmas Eve, I didn't think we was so close to the front at that place. I thought we would be back further. We could hear the shelling. We thought it was German shelling." Frank described his wounds. " Well, I've got a 2 inch by 3 and 3/4 inch steel plate in my head. My wife told everybody when I got home, she could stick her fist in my head. In my right arm, this bone is completely gone. They took part of the bone out – there was no flesh there at all. They sewed my arm to my stomach and the flesh became part of my arm. They took skin off my legs to cover my stomach. These fingers are numb – only two fingers work on my right hand. They tried to fix the nerve, but it didn't never work. But, I can move 'em more than I used to. That hole there in my arm, it didn't heal – it didn't heal, so they put a drain in there. Finally, they took a piece of bone out where it didn't heal".

We talked about the hospital at Bar-le-Duc." They put that skin graft on over there and they cut that off my thigh, too. The knives were so dull, they dug and dug in and instead of just taking skin, they took flesh and all, in some places – they just covered it up! They took skin off my legs to cover the forearm where there was no flesh left – just bones. When they put that bandage on my thigh, they didn't put enough Vaseline on. When they took that off it hurt worse than anything else. It dried up, so it stuck in! It was worse than when they took the bandage off my arm!

I left Bar-le Duc Christmas day. I was lucky, too. The doctors told me that if my head wound had been a half-inch either way, I would have been paralyzed for life. It's funny, if you get hit on the right side of your head, the left side of your body is paralyzed. They put me in an ambulance and went to the train station. All I remember is riding up the street and seeing the street lights out the back window. They put me on the train and that night just outside of Paris, we had Christmas dinner. They give us turkey gravy on toast for dinner! Then that night we got outside of Paris and the train froze up. And we sat there – I don't know how many days we sat there. Must have been a few. It was <u>so</u> cold. The guys hollered, '<u>More blankets, more blankets</u>!' - and they didn't have no more. I didn't get cold but I was hurting something terrible – I ached so!

Frank took a boat across the channel. " The 31st of December I got back to England to Litchfield, a hospital in a town not too far from Bristol. I took my first steps there. The next day or two after I got to Litchfield, the nurse said I had to shave. I said I don't think I can! She said, '<u>yes you can</u> – <u>you've got to</u>!' So I got my things and went into the bathroom and got lathered up, I got so hot, I thought I was going to pass out – I almost did! I tried to shave with my left hand. I told her I had to sit down. I stuck it out and I did it! It took me quite awhile but I finished. Oh, the nurses were good and the ward boys were good, too.

We (*The 6th Armored Div.*) arrived in England on the 22nd of February,1944 and they put me on the boat going home on the 22nd of February,1945 one year to the day. I didn't walk off or on the boat, shipping to and from England. We sailed out of Bristol on the hospital ship, The USS Charleston and we landed in Charleston, South Carolina on the 5th of March.

We just stayed there overnight. They wouldn't give me a pass, 'cuz anyone with a cast couldn't get a pass – I had a cast on my right arm. They give everybody money to call home when we landed." Can you imagine how great it was for Mary to talk to her husband again? " The next morning they put us on a train and the next night we ate supper at the Market Street Station in Philadelphia. I had a bandage on my head to cover the hole where I lost part of my skull and the left half of my ear– couldn't wear a hat. From there I went to Valley Forge General Hospital at Phoenixville – near Philadelphia. I got there that night and we had to see a doctor. The first thing he said was, " Would you like to go home?.' I said, I sure would! The doctor added, ' There's only one thing - you've got to go to a doctor in a few days and have the bandage changed. He wrote me a pass and I left for home the next morning, March 7th. He gave me a ten day pass."

Mary was living in Troy, New York, just nine miles north of Albany on the east side of the Hudson river. She was working for Montgomery Ward and also going to college at night. She stayed in the YWCA with other girls. " After Frank had called me to tell me he was coming home, I had told them in the YW where I'd be every minute, because I knew he was back in the states. When he came by train into Albany, I was eating supper with a bunch of girls. They came and told me – phone call! I talked to Frank and went back to finish my supper. I hopped up and said I have to go. They asked where are you going. I said to the railroad station in Troy - because I thought that was the best place to tell Frank how to get there from Albany on a bus. I told the girls, I have to go to the railroad station to meet my husband. I wish you could have heard the girls!

It was a little over a year since I had seen him. He wrote and told us he got injured in the arm, but I didn't know when I met him whether he was going to have an arm or not. It was a terrible feeling. The girls all wanted to go to the station with me from the Y, but I said – no way! He wasn't the strongest then and I wanted to be alone with him for a time. We walked back to the YWCA and the girls saw him there. We called his sister and she drove her car to give us a ride home to Hoosick Falls.

Frank had a strep throat and spent most of his time in bed. The family doctor came to the house. He said he couldn't treat the sore throat because it was a problem being treated by the Army. Frank responded, " Well I'm not leaving this house, I just got here. I've been gone for over a year. If you don't give me any medicine that's fine." So, the doctor left some for him and went on to dress his head wound. Just before the doctor left the house, the bandage fell off. I've never forgotten this - one of his sisters, Blanch said, don't worry about it – don't call him back. She cracked an egg and took the white of the egg, put it on the bandage, stuck it on his head and it stayed there! The white of the egg acted like glue and it stayed and never moved!"

After the pass was over, Frank took the train back to Philadelphia. " When I got back to Valley Forge General Hospital, the doc says, ' What are you doing here?. You should be over in Atlantic City'. So, they transferred me to Hadden Hall right on the Boardwalk. There were two or three hotels that they turned into hospitals. I stayed there all summer. They done that first, they put the plate in my head there in Atlantic City." Mary quit her job in Troy with Montgomery Ward and moved to Atlantic City to be with Frank. They didn't have much money so Mary got two jobs to make ends meet. She worked at a newspaper collecting ads and also typed menus for a restaurant so she got free meals. She would visit Frank after lunch and then in the evening.

" After the summer (*1945*) in Atlantic City, they shipped me back to Valley Forge. That's where they put the flesh onto my arm and ear. That's when they sewed my arm to my stomach. It took three weeks." Flesh from his stomach grew into his arm during this time. " Bar-le-Duc they just put the skin on over there – it came from my thigh and it just covered my arm. They sewed my ear back, but didn't have enough flesh to make it full. They only put on half or a little more. Both shoulders were broke and one collar bone, too. I still got one piece of shrapnel in my leg. How much more they took out in Bar-le-Duc, I don't know. My last surgery was July 1946. That was when they tried to fix this nerve" – and he points to his arm. " I was discharged on August 12, 1946. Well, I walked onto the boat in New York going to Europe, I got carried off on a stretcher in Scotland, I got carried on the hospital ship, Charleston and I walked off the boat when it landed in Charleston, South Carolina!"

And, now the question about his disability? Someone in the Army has to recognize this and give a war hero a pension for his life span. " I think it's 80%. - I never knew until this summer (*in 2000*) when I went to the VA Hospital and they looked it up. I started out with a monthly payment of $150 and over the years it has increased." Yes, the government has increased payments over the years, but it would be considered poverty level by today's standards if veterans like Frank had to depend on a disability check for a decent life. With all the political pork barrel projects that came out of Washington since 1945, one has to wonder why the USA hasn't taken better care of disabled veterans!

Frank spent some time in VA hospitals after he was discharged from the Army. I asked about the lingering effects of his wounds. " Through the years I got some spells of pain in my head. It felt like the steel plate was pressing - cutting into my flesh. It only lasted a few days and then it would go away. It probably happened only three or four times in all these years. The first time I went into a VA Hospital as an outpatient was in 1984 in Albany. I've gone back every six months where I have a lady doctor."

Frank and Mary have lived a long and rugged life farming in the Hoosick Falls area where both he and Mary grew up. They live in a 200-year old red brick historic farmhouse where relatives frequently gather. They had a family of six children, four girls and two boys. Like many returning GI's, this family suffered another terrible tragedy. In 1960, their little blonde six year old daughter, Kay, was run over by a school bus right in front of their farm home. She died in Frank's arms on the way to the hospital. This was a very difficult time for the Cipperly's – especially Frank who had been through so much!

Now it's the year 2001 – a long time away from World War II. The other five children live close by and are home often. Over the years Frank acquired additional acreage and now farms 720 acres with the help of his son, Carl. They raise corn, have a herd of Holstein cattle and even make maple syrup to sell from the maple trees on their land. The other son, Dee, lives next door and Janice, lives just a short walk away down the road. Another daughter, Betsy lives only 14 miles away while Elva works near Albany as a computer consultant, a thirty minute drive away. Elva organized a mini-reunion in September 2001 for 50th Armored Infantry Battalion veterans and their families to keep in touch with each other. The Cipperly's and their relatives are close knit Yankees!

I wonder if other generations can imagine what these combat veterans endured in World War II? I think of Frank suffering with his wounds, his battle for life --- unconscious for nineteen days ---, a shattered arm and hand, a hole in his skull, big

enough for a fist to go into, broken shoulders and collar bone and shrapnel in his body - then the healing process for almost two years with many surgeries. He is a humble happy man. The most touching thing he said during the whole interview, " I'm a very lucky man! "

Frank and Mary- November 2000 at their Hoosick Falls, New York. Home.

Frank Cipperly and Hudson Wirth celebrating Veterans Day together at the Cipperly home in Hoosick Falls, New York on November 11th , 2000.

Raymond Frank Mutz

Ray Mutz grew up in Colorado, in fact he has spent his entire life in that beautiful state except for his hitch in the U S Army in World War II. His mother and father immigrated to America from Slovenia, which most of us remember as being the very northern part of Yugoslavia. His father, Frank Louis Mutz was born in 1898. His mother, Teresa Tezak was born on Aug. 1,1898 in a neighboring village. Like many other US soldiers in World War II, *Ray was about to fight the Germans.... when his father fought in World War I with the German Army. Ray has a photo of his father in his German uniform.*

When World War I broke out in 1914, Frank Louis Mutz was a young lad of 14 years old. Later in that war, he was drafted into the German Army as a citizen of Slovenia, which was part of the Austro-Hungarian Empire at that time. He served on the Italian front and was not captured but he was wounded. After the war, he made up his mind to go to America if at all possible. He had two brothers in the United States in Pueblo, Colorado and Teresa had a sister in Joliet, Illinois.

The childhood sweethearts came to America in late 1919 to Joliet, where Teresa's relatives had settled. They were married on New Years Day, January 1, 1921. The young couple moved to Pueblo, Colorado shortly thereafter where there was a substantial Slovenian population. He got a job at the large Colorado Fuel and Iron steel plant as a die reamer used in the manufacture of wire. Frank and Teresa had their first born son, Frank William Mutz on December 12, 1921. Raymond Frank Mutz came along October 3,1925. Their folks always called Frank by his middle name, William and called Ray by his middle name Frank. Ray laughed when he told this story and then added, " My uncle, Dad's older brother, had a son named the same as me , Raymond Frank Mutz – so there were two of us in Pueblo."

The Mutz family was happy in their adopted country. They became United States citizens in a Federal Court ceremony in Denver. " When my Mother and Dad got their citizenship papers it wasn't just handed to them. You had to go to school. My Dad got his papers first and later when my Mother got hers, I was a little kid and it was a great celebration!", told Ray. They were very proud to become Americans and still participate in social activities with the local Slovenian association. The two young boys had a typical bringing up by their parents with a lot of outdoor activities, hunting, fishing, camping, ice skating, etc. Ray learned to play an accordion and was a close friend of his older brother, William. Ray recalls a time when he came home from school and called himself a ," Bojon " – slang for Slovenian. His father admonished him saying, " Don't you ever call yourself a Bojon! You are not a Bojon, you are an American!"

In 1940 his brother, William, enlisted in the Navy. The night before he was to report for duty, he was involved in a car accident. He lost 90 per cent of his vision in one eye so he was not accepted for Naval duty.

Ray graduated from Pueblo High School in June 1943. He wanted to join the Navy in the submarine service. " For some reason submarines fascinated me. I used to make models of submarines – kept magazine articles and pictures of them," Ray related. He was the right size for this since he was of slight build – 140 pounds and five feet five inches tall. In Denver at the recruitment center the candidates were given preliminary tests. One was a colorblind test. Ray didn't realize he was colorblind. Standing in line he saw the Navy person flipping two pages of dotted colors and asking the enlistees to name the number in the dots. He heard the number 39 announced by the guy ahead of him. When his test time came, he had memorized the page and answered the same question with 39. A few minutes later, Ray had a change of heart," I realized that I can't do that. Submarines have many color-coded valves, buttons and switches and I might push the wrong button." He told the Navy man that he couldn't read the number. The Navy then offered him a chance to join the C-Bees, the Navy equivalent of Army engineers but he turned that down. Ray went back to Pueblo somewhat disheartened.

On November 12, 1943, Ray received the famous draft notice (FROM THE PRESIDENT OF THE UNITED STATES: To Raymond Frank Mutz... GREETINGS....). The reception center was in downtown Denver. " And you know, in those days after you passed the physical, you were given two weeks or thirty days to go home and settle up your business and tie up the loose ends. I told my folks when I left for Denver, I ain't comin' home" said Ray. "My Dad said, you don't know what your getting into – and he was right!". It was exciting. Like other teen-agers of the era, he didn't want to be left out of World War II. Remember, the United States had just barely recovered from the Great Depression years of 1929-1938. Only the slow war buildup in 1939-40 put many people back to work. President Roosevelt had to cajole Congress to get military appropriations to build an Armed Force capable of fighting a war in Europe. Most young draftees had never traveled far from their hometowns, much less from their states!

Draftees from Colorado in this area were sent to Ft. Logan, just outside of Denver, west of Littleton. By the time Ray's contingent were sworn into the Army and got their papers, it was 10 o'clock at night. The new recruits marched to the barracks and were assigned bunks. " I'll never forget as I laid there in the dark, I could hear some of the people crying. What's goin' on here I thought ", Ray related and then added, " Boy, did they have a rude awakening the next morning when they blew that whistle! We ran outside and it was still dark. There were a couple of guys that just sauntered out a little bit slow – still in their civilian clothes. You could barely see a water tower a long distance away. The First Sergeant. had another noncom take those guys on a double-time march to the water tower and back, before their first Army roll call." You're in the Army now! You're not behind the plow...!

From there Ray was sent to Ft. Knox, Kentucky for 17 weeks of basic Armored training. There he qualified as a medium tank 75-mm gunner for the M4 Sherman tank. The 34-ton Sherman came from designs of the 1930's and was hastily brought into mass production in 1942 after Pearl Harbor. It had a crew of five soldiers, two drivers in the front, the gunner and ammunition loader in the turret. The tank commander stood in the upper part of the turret so he could see out, either with the hatch open or through a periscope when it was closed. The 75 mm cannon, with 2000 foot muzzle velocity per second, was copied from the French artillery piece of World War I. The engine was a Ford Motor Company 500 horsepower V-8, rear mounted, producing a top speed of 26 miles per hour. While it was faster than the German tanks, the Sherman was generally regarded as under armored and under powered to contest Panzer tanks armed with more powerful 76 mm and 88mm high velocity cannons.

The Sherman had a 30-caliber machine gun that was mounted on the turret and moved with the 75-mm cannon. So, the gunner could fire both the machine gun and the cannon simultaneously. Just what does a tanker do to fire his weapons? " What you could do is fire the machine gun and watch where the tracer bullets went and then fire the loaded cannon at the same target. The firing mechanism was just like two floorboard dimmer switches for headlights on old cars – one switch for the machine gun and the other for the cannon - right next to each other. You could move your feet quickly from one to the other," according to Ray.

For sighting other than tracers, Ray remembers, " We had a telescopic sight that covered both eyes. This gave us our elevation, which was cranked up or down strictly by hand to aim the cannon. You could turn the turret either by hand for a minor adjustment or electrically faster by moving a shovel handle-like lever right or left. This was one feature of the Sherman tank over the Panzers which traversed slowly – only by hand. For target practice we shot three rounds of armor piercing shells at sheets moving sideways on a track out about 200 yards ahead of us."

After finishing basic training at Ft. Knox in March 1944, Ray got a 10 day furlough before moving on to Fort Meade, Maryland for about two weeks. Like hoards of other troops heading overseas, he was sent to a port of embarkation, Camp Kilmer, New Jersey in early May. He went over on the troopship "New Amsterdam", unescorted at full speed, in order to out run any German U-boats.

They landed at Grenoc, Scotland and then traveled by train to Frome, England. "While I was at Frome, they took us one time to a British post to shoot tank 75mm cannons. We passed through the town of Minehead, which was across the bay from Wales. We were shooting at targets a couple of hundred yards out. If you missed, the shells went out into the ocean", Ray said. In late 1943 and early 1944, American troops were pouring into the British Isles as fast as possible for the buildup for D-Day which was originally scheduled for early May. The Yankees descended on the south of England, some lived in English quarters. They dated the English girls and of course aggravated the English lads. The popular phrase describing the situation by the Limeys was, 'Americans were over-paid, over-sexed and over-here!'. The American troop response, was,' the British lads were under-sexed, under-paid and under Eisenhower!'

General Eisenhower made his decision to set the date for D-Day on June 5, 1944. Stormy weather caused a one-day delay to the 6th of June. That terrible battle has been written about in detail by many great historians. Movies have been made depicting the awful carnage. Those of us who weren't there can not imagine the utter chaos and agony of the gallant soldiers who fought so bravely there. Perhaps other soldiers who have been under direct enemy fire can relate to what happened on the Normandy beaches – especially at Omaha beach. With the enormous casualties in the first week of fighting, the task of getting replacements to the front developed quickly.

The Yanks in Great Britain began their journey to replace their killed and wounded comrades in France. Ray crossed the English Channel a short time after D-Day. He landed at Omaha Beach, which had been cleared for landing by that time but still was cluttered with the destruction of war. Nearing the beach, they went over the side of the ship on a landing net, transferring into a small Higgins landing craft. Soldiers had to cling to the nets like monkeys. With rough seas in the English Channel, each man had to time his final jump into the landing craft. A miss could cause one to get squeezed to death between ships or drown in the sea with the heavy weight of all their combat gear causing them to sink.

He was a qualified medium tank gunner replacement. He climbed up the draws of the Omaha beach area moving to a tent camp of 400-500 soldiers in a field not far inland and close enough to hear artillery duels. The problem was, they didn't need many medium tank gunner replacements because most of the armored divisions didn't land until about the middle of July. As the Normandy lodgment area increased in size, armor could be unloaded. The 6th Armored Division left England on July 18,1944 and by July 24th the last of the division personnel and supplies had been unloaded on Utah beach on the Cherbourg peninsula.

The Allies were hemmed in a very narrow area of Normandy until the St. Lo breakthrough on July 25th, 1944. On July 27th elements of the 6th Armored Division moved onto the attack in a southerly direction. On August 1,1944, the Third US Army was formed under the command of Gen. George Patton. He sent his 4th and 6th Armored Divisions through the hole in the German lines, directing the 6th Armored to veer west through Brittany to seal off or capture the port of Brest. Meanwhile the 4th Armored was ordered to continue south through the gap toward Rennes and the French port of Lorient on the Brittany peninsula.

While Ray's division was racing toward Brest, the replacements were moving farther into France from one Reppo Deppo (replacement depot) to another. By August 12th, the 6th Armored Division was successful in sealing off the port of Brest, which was defended by about 40,000 German troops in a semi-circle fortress-like defensive position. By August 14th, Gen. Patton was anxious to move his Third Army Armored divisions rushing east to help trap the Germans caught in the Falaise gap. Patton left one combat command , Combat Command A to contain the Brest area until relieved by the 2nd Infantry Division. He sent the rest of the division toward Lorient to relieve the 4th Armored Division. He wasn't one to sit back and wait for others to attack the German Army. He wanted to get going toward Le Mans and the Seine River and Paris.

On Sept. 5th, the 6th Armored Division received orders placing it in Army Reserve. This was an opportunity to reassemble the whole division, which had been scattered across some 250 miles of the Brittany peninsula. It had been a daring dash ...a 10,000 man armored division slicing Brittany in two , disrupting German communications, supplies and capturing 6,270 enemy soldiers. Somewhere this division needed time to replace their killed in action, wounded and missing. They also needed to be supplied with gasoline and ammunition. During this time, Ray joined his outfit before they got to Nancy, France.

Ray tells his story, " We were near some little French town in a replacement tent camp. We (*another soldier friend*) decided to go into town to have a good time. When we got back to the replacement depot, there was nothing there except our gear lying on the grass. Now, I thought, we really are in trouble! A Sergeant said you guys are scheduled to go to the 6th Armored Division. So, they loaded us in a jeep and dropped us off at the command post – where you don't know anyone – and they don't know who you are at this time. A 6th Armored Sergeant said, ' We've got all of our tanker replacements. We don't need you in the tanks anymore. Under, I'm not sending you back! You're going to the 50th Armored Infantry Battalion' (*1,000 men at full compliment – which wasn't often*). I thought to myself, well you messed up, you got to pay the consequences. But then,

67

after I saw what those 88's were doing to our tanks, I says, this Sgt. knows what he wants, I better take care of him!"

Ray was assigned to Company B, 2nd platoon, 1st rifle squad with Sgt. Joe Cybor as squad leader who had already earned a Silver Star medal for bravery in the Brest peninsula campaign. Lloyd Moore from Orofino, Idaho joined the squad the same day. Another soldier in the rifle squad was Oakie A. Morris from the hills of West Virginia – his mailing address was New Martinsville c/o General Delivery. He was the oldest member of the squad and the biggest character. Oakie was also the half-track driver. Pfc. Brady was from Ohio and John Gettel from Hagerstown, Maryland. There were others from coast to coast in the USA. Ray said, "We became a group. You know, really, if I had to do it over again, I still think I'd go back in the Infantry. I can't remember, even when I was taking basic – I never did see arguments. It was just like - we're all in the same boat. And, never in the same outfit did I see two guys really get mad at each other." Young soldiers bonded quickly to one another – their lives depended on each other!

From World War II history we know that in August,1944, the German 7th Army, upon direct orders from Hitler, planned an attack to move west from Mortain toward Avranches on the coast. This would have cut the American forces in the St. Lo breakthrough in half. The plan was to isolate the two armored divisions that crashed through to Brittany and cut off the troops in the Cherbourg peninsula. The attack began August 7,1944 under the direction of German Field Marshall von Kluge. Germany's top three Panzer divisions rolled to the west. The valiant 30th Infantry Division held their ground in the Mortain area against overwhelming odds. By August 11th the Nazi attack was stalled. In the meantime, the Allied High Command, saw a chance to encircle the Germans. Patton was sent scurrying to the south, then east, then north to Argentan to trap the huge 7th German Army. Gen. Montgomery directed the British and Canadian Armies to drive south from Caen toward Falaise to meet the American pincer moving north.

Some military plans work and this one did to an extent. This battle is known as the Falaise Gap. The German Army was caught in a huge trap and decimated - even though Montgomery failed to close the gap. The Germans were trapped in a narrow pocket and attempted to escape to the east and establish a defensive line near the

Seine river before Paris. The German Army was slaughtered in a chaotic retreat through an eleven mile gap. The British, Canadians and Polish pounded them from the north. The Americans squeezed them from the west and south and the Air Force finished the job bombing and strafing columns fleeing through the narrow pincer. On the 19th of August, Field Marshall von Kluge was relieved of his command by Hitler. Since he was involved in the July 20th assassination attempt on Adolph Hitler in east Germany, he was a marked man. He wrote a letter to Hitler appealing for an end to the war. Then he took a cyanide pill committing suicide. Gen. Eisenhower, upon inspection at the end of the battle, said this scene of the remains of the German Army was the worst destruction of men and equipment he ever saw. While some 100,000 to 150,000 German soldiers escaped to the east toward Germany, about 10,000 were killed and 50,000 were captured. As they fled, they left their horse drawn artillery, heavy equipment and tanks behind them.

On August 29th, the American 28th Infantry Division marched triumphantly through the Arc de Triumph in Paris. Gen. De Gaulle had engineered the parade to gather support for his political power and to gain approval of the French people as the liberator of France. He was fighting for political control of France against a strong Communist party. Brussels was liberated on September 2nd. What remained of the German Army in France fled to the shelter of the German border and the Westwall or Siegfried line. Meanwhile, German war production hit an all-time high in November of 1944 - in spite of all the bombing by the British and American Air Forces. The Allied supply lines were stretched several hundred miles from the beaches and Eisenhower needed a seaport. He directed Gen. Montgomery to get Antwerp for a harbor. This attack was slowed by Monty's disastrous Garden Market offensive in early September when he tried to cross the lower Rhine river at Arnheim in Holland. Antwerp was not captured until November 8, 1944 and the Schelde estuary was opened later so that supply ships could get past to unload upstream in Antwerp. Winter set in and the hope the war could end before long was dashed.

By the fall of 1944, American troops were far east of Paris. The 6th Armored division was one of the divisions that kept the pressure on the German Army, which had retreated close to or into the German border. This distance from the Atlantic coast, shortened their supply lines while at the same time lengthening the Allies supply lines.

Throughout September, October and November, the 6th Armored Division was fighting in the area of Nancy and Metz, France. These cities are located about 150 air miles directly east of Paris and only 25 to 40 miles from the German border city of Saabrucken. At times, elements of the Division were fighting only 20 miles east of Verdun, the site in 1916 of one of the longest and most deadly battles in World War I. German resistance stiffened closer to the Fatherland. Americans, mired down by the lack of supplies, ammunition and gasoline, made little progress in destroying the German Army. The weather was cold, rainy and muddy. Casualties continued to mount on both sides.

Ray tells this sad story of one of his squad members. Pfc. Brady was wounded near the Seille River – shot in the arm. The 6th Armored Division had met up with the 7th US Army coming up from the south of France from the August 14th invasion near Marseilles called operation Anvil. It was now fighting a campaign near the German border. Patton had run out of gas. Most of the supplies had gone to Gen. Montgomery for his campaigns in Holland, much to Patton's ire. Ray recalled this story, " Brady got shot in the arm and it broke the bone. We told him - Hey! You've got a million dollar wound because they're going to send you home since the bone is shattered. A couple of weeks later, we heard he died - went into shock or something like that. He's not in our book as killed in action, since he was wounded and died a couple of weeks later in a hospital."

Ray told how he was made assistant half-track driver, " I had machine gun training in Ft. Knox. When I took basic, besides being a gunner on a tank, we drove everything - all kinds of vehicles, tanks, half-tracks and trucks. So, when I went to the 50th Arm'd. Inf. Bn., Co. B they made me Oakie Morris' assistance driver." His job changed from being a 75 mm cannon gunner in a Sherman tank to manning a 50-caliber machine gun attached to half-track # 47.

Oakie A. Morris was the oldest member in this squad of 12 soldiers – 12 men when filled up with replacements, which wasn't often. He was also the squad character and probably learned to like moonshine from local stills back home in the hollows of West Virginia. Ray told this story about Oakie. Since they spent a good deal of time together around the half-track, they got to know each other very well. One day in October, Oakie unhappily told Ray, "I'm one of the oldest guys in the company and I got

70

a pass to Paris, but I ain't got no money." Ray said, " Oakie, I've got some money. How much do you need?" Oakie replied, " Well, a couple hundred dollars." "OK," said Ray. So, he loaned Oakie the money. Now, this was a lot since the monthly pay for a private was $ 75.00 dollars a month. If you were a PFC (*private first class*) with a Combat Infantry Badge you were paid an extra ten dollars or $85 per month. In order to earn a Combat Infantry Badge, you had to cross the line of demarcation in an attack on an enemy position. That's why those blue badges are so prized. Oakie was told by his officer that he'd better be back right after his pass was over. Oakie didn't show up for two weeks! Ray said, " When he come back to the outfit from Paris, he was a disgrace to the US Army! He looked like a bum. He run out of money. He hocked his watch to get money and sold his GI overcoat. They broke him one rank from a T-5 to PFC for one month." Thinking that was the last that Ray ever saw of his money, he was asked, "Did you ever get paid back?" Ray laughingly replied, " You wouldn't believe it. About two weeks after Oakie got back to the squad, he wasn't feeling any pain and got in a crap game somewhere. And, he paid me back plus some."

On December 16, 1944, the Battle of the Bulge (*the Ardennes as the Germans called it*) broke out. Hitler had presented his plan to his top staff of Generals in Wolfshanze (*wolfs lair*) in September 1944 at his East Prussian headquarters. The strategy called for a surprise massive Panzer attack through a sparsely defended area in the most hilly, forested terrain of Belgium and Luxembourg. The offensive was designed to split the American and the British Armies in two, make a powerful dash across the Meuse River, sweep on to Antwerp, Belgium, and then carve up each army separately. For the point of his attack west, Hitler used the " Losheim Gap", just north of Luxembourg, near the Belgian towns of Malmedy and St. Vith. This is the exact area the Germans were so successful in World War I and again in May,1940 in the Blitzkrieg of France, when the Panzers did an end run around the almost impregnable Maginot line.

For this offensive, the Germans had 1427 combat ready tanks and had refitted three large armies, which included seven armored divisions and thirteen infantry divisions. Facing this German attack were four American divisions scattered over a front of 110 km or 68 miles. In addition, Hitler's generals had assembled 3420 artillery guns for this winter "Blitzkrieg". The GI's were outnumbered in many of the attack points by ten to one.

The 6th Armored Division was fighting near Sarreguemines, France when the Battle of the Bulge began. This French town is just across the Saar River, the border between France and the German city of Saarbrucken. Gen. Patton was asked to pivot his 3rd Army which was facing east and rush it north to Bastogne to relieve the heroic defenders of that Belgian town, where the 101st Airborne Div. and a combat command of the 10th Armored Div. were surrounded. Patton anticipated this command. On Dec. 19th he had his Staff prepare for Bastogne. His 4th and 6th Armored Divisions hurried north some 80 miles. The 101st Airborne was asked to surrender to the Germans just before Christmas when Gen. McAuliffe gave his famous reply to the German ultimatum, "Nuts!" Today, in a tradition, when St. Nicholas comes down the street of Bastogne during their Christmas parade, he tosses nuts to little children as a symbol honoring American soldiers who liberated them. On December 26th tankers and infantry of CCR of the 4th Armored broke through the German ring to relieve the Americans trapped there since December 18th.

The Germans dropped propaganda leaflets behind the American lines in an effort to get the Yanks to surrender. Hitler thought the GI's were weaker than his prize Panzer divisions – especially since they outnumbered the Americans at this stage of the battle. Ray kept one leaflet that he picked up.

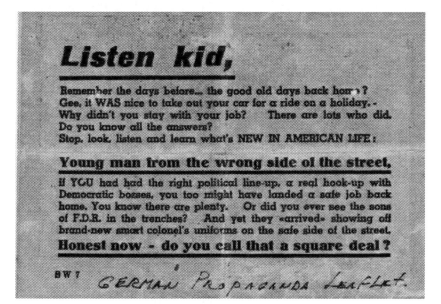

The 6th Armored Division was in position by December 30th to start an attack north and east of Bastogne with the 35th Infantry Division on its right flank. These roads led to a series of small hamlets which became famous as the sites of giant struggles by two massive armies. Some say the weather was the worst winter in 100 years... snowy and freezing cold. For the next two weeks the foes were locked in battle around Bastogne. Hitler issued a priority command that this major crossroad should be taken at all costs. Casualties on both sides mounted.

" We had another young replacement , a little bitty guy like myself," said Ray." In fact he was smaller and he'd been a jockey for the comedian Joe E. Lewis. When we tried to take that little town east of Bastogne, I was staying with Oakie Morris since I was the half-track machine gunner. I'll never forget a long snow field and trees. On our left there was a half-track, a tank and then another tank. We unloaded the squad and they walked across this field towards these trees. All hell broke loose. I had a water cooled machine gun and I sprayed the trees trying to give them cover. I burned the barrel up. Pretty soon I had to stop shooting because the tracers were going all over- when you lose the rifling of the barrel. A tank got hit. Then the next tank got hit. Then the half-track next to us got hit. I said to Oakie, I don't care what you do but move! Don't sit here like a pigeon. So, we circled around in that field. About that time the troops started coming back. This kid that was the jockey, they got him back into the half-track. He had a big chunk of his leg missing and was hit in the other thigh, too. We got him back to the aid station and of course he was covered with a blanket. I asked him how he's doing. He didn't know how bad his legs were. He couldn't have been with us a week. He said ,'I don't feel nothin' in my legs.' Honest to God, I swear he wasn't with us a week and he was gone!

When Oakie and I was sitting in that half-track, when we were starting to pull out, I saw this one GI running across this field. A shell must have hit right at his feet. I swear to God, I could see him start to rise up and then just disappear. There was a guy by the name of Montgomery, in B Company, but not in our squad. His last name was Montgomery 'cause they reported him as missing. Three or four weeks later some officer came to us. We had to verify what happened." His name was Pfc. Homer C. Montgomery. Many times MIA's (*missing in action*) meant a horrible scene of battle similar to this where there are not enough body parts left to identify a soldier. Veterans never forget these scenes – this one is etched in Ray's mind after all these years!

By January 12th, Ray's squad had been in their snowy foxholes for three or four days. That night his friend and squad leader, Sgt. William G. Irwin shared a foxhole with Ray. Irwin was apprehensive about the next day. He told Ray, " I got a feeling, something terrible is going to happen tomorrow." Irwin told Ray a little bit about his family. He was the only child and the only grandchild. Ray said, " That's when I told him, the Army had a policy that if you were the only survivor, you can get out of combat – they'd assign you a job in the rear echelon. But, Irwin declined to do that – he just wouldn't do that!" (see map in Web Halvorsen chapter)

On the 13th of January 1945, Ray's 50th Armored Inf. Bn. was in an attack position heading from the tiny town of Bizory toward the hamlet Mageret. Ray's job was in half-track # 47 on the machine gun with Oakie Morris, the driver. When it came time to move out, Ray describes the situation, " We was near a little house in Bizory. We didn't start from Bizory on foot 'til 12 or 1 o'clock in the afternoon – 'cuz it's just over the hill. Lloyd Moore was just like this - (Ray demonstrates how soldiers on the verge of a breakdown start to shake). Lloyd, I says, I'll tell you what. You stay with Oakie and I'll fill in for you. So, that's when I got shot up. But, I could tell, he was in bad shape. Little did I know I was going to get hit. Actually, that Heinie done me a favor with a flesh wound." Then Ray laughed in his usual jovial manner, "I got out of the snow and the cold weather!"

He added, " When you come to Mageret, the town was over a ridge. There was a long hedgerow and we were going right into that hedge. Sgt. Irwin was near the hedge row when he went down. Oakie later told me that they helped pick up the bodies the next day with the half-tracks. He said he didn't recognize Irwin at first. He got hit in the temple, the nose and the bottom of his jaw – by a machine gun! I never knew he was killed until Oakie told me later. I don't know whether I got hit by a stray machine gun bullet, a sniper or what. Irwin was the squad leader and I was the assistant squad leader. That was the first time I went with him 'cuz I was taking Moore's place. The half-tracks stayed back at Bizory – we were just walking.". Usually the half-tracks would move with the squad and provide machine cover into the hedge rows if possible. " When

I first got shot, I thought somebody was behind me, because I didn't feel the slug when it went in but when it come out. It knocked me down and I turned my head around to see who was behind me." The bullet entered his left thigh and came out near the lower part of his buttocks.

Ray's story went on, " After I got hit, I'm laying in the snow, and here comes a tank – one of our tanks - about 25 yards from me - going toward the hedges. There was some GI right behind the tail of the tank, right close to the edge of the tank, close behind it. That tank got hit by a Panzerfaust (*German bazooka*) on the tail end of the deck and didn't do no damage- I think it knocked off one of the Cat Eyes (*small driving light*). This soldier went down like a ton of bricks – he didn't move. That tank kept on going. I laid in the snow. I think our first aid man was a guy by the name of Chambers, Chandler or something. He come by and I told him I'm all right. Go help somebody else. He went to raise this one kid up who was shot through the chest. The medic was kneeling down to wrap a bandage around his chest - it must have been a sniper that killed that medic." Our 50th Armored Infantry records show Harold E. Chambers killed in action – all our medics were unarmed and wore a helmet with white circle and Red Cross in the center which was clearly visible to the enemy. These medics were the brave!

" I really can't explain how I felt – I knew I was shocked. The bullets were still whistling around, so I crawled over to where the tank had traveled and lay in one of the snow tracks to get lower in the field. I just laid there and pretty soon there's no more tanks and no more troops. I could see some guys laying in the snow. What shape they were in, I didn't know. I laid there and laid there and nobody came and it's getting dark." In Belgium at this latitude, it gets dark by 4:00 P.M. in the wintertime. Ray said, " I laid there, it must have been 9 o'clock and I said to myself, I'm not going to freeze to death. I heard some tanks idling off in the distance to our rear, so I got up and started hobbling towards them tanks. I run across some GI – I had no idea who he was. He said,' please help me '. I said, I can't help you right now, but I'll guarantee one thing, I'll get somebody back here to help you. I kept on walking and sure enough, I ran into our tanks and they didn't even know we were in this field. When I come to this tank – these guys were great. A medic came and I got behind the tank under the engine where it was warm and they covered me with a blanket. I told them to follow my tracks down through that snow.

There's a fellow down there in bad shape and there's some other wounded people in that field, too.

They went and got two guys out. Now whether they got the GI who asked me for help, I don't know. They wanted to put me on a stretcher – you know they could handle two stretchers on a Jeep. I said no, I'll catch the next one. I'm all right, I'm fine. Soon, they come back with another Jeep and I got out. They took me to a hospital and I lost all track of time. It must have been one or two o'clock in the morning, but I remember they took me into this tent and just put the stretcher right on saw horses. There were quite a few of us in there. I was only there that night' 'cuz they cut on me that night or in the morning." These times usually became a little fuzzy since standard procedure was to give the wounded a shot of morphine to kill the pain.

Ray carried a letter from his brother, Bill, in his pants pocket. The return address reads - "WAR DEPARTMENT - OFFICIAL BUSINESS U.S. V MAIL." It was dated Dec. 25,1944 from Portland, Oregon. Messages were written on V-Mail paper, then microfilmed to reduce the size to 4 inches by 5 inches. The Army V-MAIL date is 6 Jan 1945. Even V-MAIL took two to three weeks during the war to reach combat troops in Europe. Ray has the original letter with blood stains from his wound.

The letter reads:

"Hello Uncle Ray:

Well, Frankie you are an uncle to a 7 lbs. 11oz. Girl, we got just what we wanted. Boy, I sure wish you could see her – she is fat and looks just like Evelyn. She was born at12:05 Dec. the 24th. We named her Theresa Ann. To you that name is nice – we named her after both of our Mothers. And if it would have been a boy I was going to name it after you. But it was a girl. You ought to see her, well she's just a roll of fat thats all. Well, I hope you are home next Xmas. And Frankie take care of yourself. I guess your right where the Germans started there push. About Sedan. That's where I guessed you were at. Well, God be with you and please take care.

Bill, Evelyn and Theresa"

" The very next night (Jan.14th) they loaded me on an ambulance, four of us in an ambulance," Ray continued. " I didn't know where we were going. We drove a long, long time. I think it was near Paris when they opened the back door of the ambulance. Your head is toward the back door – who opened the door but a Kraut and another Kraut who is in uniform." Ray laughed heartily, " I thought the driver went the wrong way! I was in that hospital in Paris about a week. Then they took me out of Paris and put me on a medical train that was headed for the coast. They had everybody on that train - people that was going to go to the coast and on home. But, us guys that had flesh wounds, they stayed on the train to LeMans.

In LeMans, they took us off to a field hospital in tents. It was nice. In that ward they must have had about 30 guys in a tent – double rows of beds – big pot bellied stoves in there. They had one 12 by 12 tent in the back for a latrine. And, I stayed there 'til I came back to the squad. When I got in the hospital, the doctor would come and look and change the bandage. He'd take it off and I could see the gauze in the center of the wound. He'd take that off with tweezers and he said your starting to heal up real good. Then he just pulled that gauze right out of the hole. The skin was starting to form around the hole – it didn't bleed or nothin' - it just grew back. The only thing it did was cut some of the nerves in my leg."

The Field Hospital with wooden floor tents in LeMans really was in a field just outside town. Ray describes what it was like, " Of course, the doctors would come to see me every day in the morning, just like they would do in any hospital. After a couple of weeks, he wanted me to walk to the latrine tent. They dressed the wound every day. This is kind of humorous. Some guys could get out of bed and walk. – We had a mess tent, too. All the cooks were German prisoners of war (POW's) – the only GI there was the Master Sergeant cook in charge. When they shut down the kitchen at night, there was nobody there. We had a couple of guys that would go over there at night, go in the kitchen and confiscate pork chops, bread and whatever food looked good. The head nurse, I don't remember her name, but she was from Iron Mountain, Michigan, and she was sweet! She collected from the other nurses – three or four mess kits. Every night we'd cook a meal on these pot-bellied iron stoves – and the nurses would join us! We'd have a feast about ten o'clock at night, " Ray then laughed loudly recalling this time.

He went on, " Another part that was funny, of course, we didn't have no uniforms. When you went in the hospital you were stripped and it's amazing how the GI's could adapt. I guess LeMans was three miles away from the tent hospital. Some of the soldiers got in trouble. The MP's (*military police*) picked them up – they didn't have no papers, no nothin'. Come to find out, they were hospital patients. But, somehow, they got hold of uniforms. They had a search at the hospital - I forget how many uniforms they turned up. The guys would get their hidden uniforms out, dress up and go into LeMans for a night on the town. So, they confiscated all the hidden uniforms. " What did the GI's wear in the hospital? Ray said without hesitation, " Pajamas and a robe which was a deep blue Army robe and we had our shoes. After I got up and could move around, there was about three or four of us – every day about one o'clock - we would go to a little crossroads about a half-mile away. There was a small French tavern there. We used to go there every day in our pajamas and robe and get back in time for chow! Well, they wanted us to walk!"

How did they determine when to send the wounded back to their units? Ray described his case," I was walking a little better each day and when the doctor made his rounds and checked the wound, he could see it was healing up. It looked like the skin was starting to close over the hole. One day he asked how I was feeling and I said okay - no pain. The only thing was some numbness in the back of my leg. The doctor said, ' I guess we'll send you back to the outfit.' They had a little bulletin board there and my name was on it – said you're free to go back! By this time it was late March. But, at first sending the wounded back became a big problem. After they recuperated, they would just send them back to the first outfit that needed a replacement. This caused a lot of guys to go over the hill (*AWOL- absent without leave*). They said, I don't mind going back, but I want to go back to the same outfit! So, they made a rule that you went back to the same outfit you came from."

79

After the Battle of the Bulge ended about January 27th, the two Armies were in a stalemate as the Germans once again got behind their protective Westwall or Siegfried line. The fighting from January 27th to March 8, 1945 was called the Dasburg, Germany to Prum River campaign by the 6th Armored Division. Both armies needed replacements, ammunition and repairs to equipment. Ray's outfit, the 50th Armored Infantry Battalion had punched through the Siegfried line beginning the 20th of February. The 6th Armored Division, along with other elements of Patton's Third Army, pushed through a narrow gap, to a distance of some 15 miles into Germany arriving at Lunebach on the Prum River. On March 4th the 6th Armored Div. was relieved by the 90th Infantry Div. The 6th Armored was directed to secretly move south some 145 miles to Luneville, France. All division insignia was removed from equipment, vehicles and including shoulder patches of the soldiers. It was being attached to the 7th Army to have another shot at breaking through the Siegfried line a second time.

On March 15th, the entire division was assembled on a beautiful sunny hill outside Luneville with a view of the Seille River valley where the division had fought in the Fall months. We had a memorial service for our wounded and fallen comrades. Then the General staff, by means of a large chart, outlined our course of action for the next campaign. This was the first time we had any idea of what might happen next and the war strategy explained to us!

Oakie A. Morris at wars end

This is the time Raymond Mutz rejoined his squad and half-track # 47 band of soldiers. " A dozen or so left the hospital at the same time," said Ray. "They put us on a train and we went back through Paris. I don't think we were 20 minutes in the depot in Paris and we pulled out. From where the train stopped, we ended up in a 2 ½ ton truck and the first thing I knew, I was back in the 6th Armored Division." The French had the railroad networks running well again. Ray told this humorous incident, " When I got back to the squad and half-track #47, I climbed in to look at my musette bag to check for the souvenirs that I accumulated – including a German Luger pistol. My bag was empty.

I says, Oakie what happened to all the stuff I had in my musette bag? Oakie shuffled his feet, hunched his shoulders, moved his lips but didn't say anything. I says, come on Oakie what happened? Oakie finally replied, 'I didn't think you wuz comin' back so I traded the stuff for two bottles of whiskey!" Ray let out a hearty laugh and then said, "That Oakie, he was a piece of cake!" Then in a very sober tone, Ray asked Oakie where William Irwin was. It was at this time Ray learned his friend, Sgt. Irwin, was KIA (*killed in action*) the same day he was wounded January 13, 1945.

On March 20[th,] when the bridgehead through the Siegfried line was established by the 3rd & 45th Infantry Divisions of the XV Corps... the 6th Armored took off in the direction of Zweibrucken, Germany. The Third Army was driving <u>southeast</u> from the northern Luxembourg German border area toward the Rhine. The 6th Armored Division with the 7th Army drove <u>northeast</u> in a pincer movement toward the Rhine River. These two Armies encircled about 200,000 German troops in the Palatinate region of Germany – between the Moselle and Rhine Rivers. The Germans were cut off from their supplies and communication. It was chaos for them with these powerful forces roaming behind their lines! On March 21st, the 6th Armored Division reached the Rhine at the famous city of Worms. This 2000 year old city, founded by the Romans, was literally untouched by the ravages of war – thereby preserving the Romanesque Cathedral where Martin Luther in 1521 defended his position on Protestantism.

Because Ray was an assistant driver, he had some training as a DUKW driver. These amphibious vehicles, called " Ducks " by the GI's, were going to be used to cross the Rhine. That never materialized because the 6th Arm'd. crossed the Rhine on a pontoon bridge at Oppenheim on March 25th. Ray talked about some of the fighting in the Palatinate area before the Rhine," I remember coming back and they said Lloyd Moore was second scout. He was the only guy that I really knew in our rifle squad before I was wounded. The rest were replacements. So, I said I would take the lead scout.

I remember the mountainous area - the column stopped and they said scouts out. Lloyd and I went up on the hill just below the crest. He was standing maybe twenty yards to the left down below me. I sat down and had the binoculars scanning. Lloyd told me to look across the canyon. All of a sudden Lloyd started shooting up the hill from the hip. I just fell on the ground and turned around. I saw these two Germans go over the top of the rise. Lloyd told me he was watching across the canyon and when he looked up, he saw one of the Germans had a bead on my shoulders. He started shooting from the hip and those two Germans turned around and ran like crazy or they would have shot me. So, Lloyd done me a favor there ,too!. Then we saw a couple of Germans coming up a trail on the other side of the ridge and they must have heard the shooting. They ducked down in the bushes. Lloyd Moore and I shot. This white flag comes down and they come walking over. There was this good looking blonde German kid...he left his helmet there and we had hit him. We took him back down to the column and they put this German kid in the ambulance. There were only two Germans and one we shot up pretty bad. – but, he walked out of there and I don't think he lived. You know, that it's actually hard to see a person you actually shot at and see him face to face. It gave me a funny feeling... when you shoot at them from a distance you don't think of them as a human being until you see them close. But, of course they are another human being just like you are." Close Combat - that is what you call eyeball to eyeball contact with the enemy as described in the fine book by Colonel James S. Moncrief Jr. Ret. " As You Were, Soldier".

The 6th Armored Division crossed the Rhine River on the 25th of March 1945 at Oppenheim, just south of Frankfurt. Engineers had erected a single lane pontoon bridge while the 5th and 90th Infantry Divisions held a narrow bridgehead on the eastern shore. In a typical Gen. Patton drive, he poured his armor across as fast as possible. He especially wanted to beat Monty across the Rhine. He wanted to keep driving and not let the enemy set up a defensive line. Using this strategy, he believed the casualties would be lower. The 6th Armored crossed on a one lane pontoon bridge in record time - 14 hours of non-stop bumper to bumper vehicles waved on by MP's. Imagine a 14 hour parade of vehicles? That will give you an idea of the size of just one armored division. The division then headed northeast toward Frankfurt.

Ray remembered another incident at this time laughing out loud before beginning, " I remember crossing the Rhine late in the daytime and after across we bivouacked in a field alongside these railroad yards. The next morning we looked over and there was a string of boxcars with no engine. We didn't know how long we was going to be there, but, we decided to walk over to the boxcars and start looking in the train. Evidently it was a German booty train that they were planning on pulling back into Germany. But, jumping the Rhine River sort of caught them 'cold turkey' and they didn't have a chance to put an engine on. We started opening the box cars to see what was in there and it was a booty train. There was machinery in there, clothing, silk stockings. Then we opened up another boxcar and we hit the jackpot – it was loaded with French booze. We loaded ourselves with bottles taking them back to the half-track. We dug holes under the ammunition in back of the seats and stuck the booze in there. When we pulled out of there, Captain Silver, who liked his liquor, got wind of it and hung around our half-track. He said, ' I hear you boys got hold of some liquor'. We said, ' We did, but we're not giving you any!" Ray ended this anecdote with another hearty laugh.

The French liquor must have lasted until the end of the war, because no one dared to drink anything during the fighting. One needed all his senses and reflexes to stay out of trouble. The officers had their own rations of liquor, so half-track # 47 became a popular supply line with the other soldiers after the war. Ray said, "Capt. Silver left Company B shortly afterward – I don't know whether it was from alcohol or combat fatigue. Soon, Capt. Haber, who was wounded, returned to take command of Company B."

The 6th Armored Division drove northeast of Frankfurt and crossed the Main River near Offenbach on March 26th. This was the first bridgehead north of Frankfurt - taken by heavy fighting. Once the division got across the Main River, it sped quickly up the Autobahn toward Kassel. There is a famous World War II photo of thousands of defeated German soldiers marching south down the Autobahn while 6th Armored columns are heading north. The end of the war was near, but there was still some heavy fighting left for another six weeks.

Company B was stalled at a little town named Malsfeld, just south of Kassel. The Fulda River ran through the middle of the town. Bridges had been blown so another attack was in order. Ray relates this episode, " I remember running towards the town. Matt Peterson was ahead of me and I caught up with him. Matt says, 'I'm tired, I can't run much further, I'm worn out.' I passed him up and as I went by him, I had my rifle on my shoulder and of course you're jogging. The bayonet guard must have got into my trigger and my rifle went off just as I went by him. Matt passed me up like I was standing still! He didn't know it was from my rifle, but he sure took off in a hurry!" Ray ended with another of his great laughs. Then he said soberly, " I remember being in that barn with John Axelson and Howard Ostrom. I remember talking to them. I left them for what reason, I don't know. I went into this house and opened a drawer in this room and here is this camera. It was a German Agfa with the old bellows you opened up. That's the camera I used to take the pictures I have. When we got to Eisenberg, there was a film factory there and I got 35 or 40 rolls of 120 film." Some of these photos are shown in this book.

The platoon spent Easter Sunday, April 1,1945, in Malsfeld. "We went to a church service in a little white German church outside of town." The Chaplain's prayers helped the guys through their sadness. War doesn't stop for sadness – it just keeps pushing on!

Armored columns of combat teams were driving east toward the old German city of Weimar. Ray told the story of being strafed by German planes, " Two columns of tanks, half-tracks, recon vehicles, tank destroyers, trucks and every vehicle in the division were moving along two parallel ridges. I was in the half-track shootin' at that Junkers 88 (*JU 88 was a twin engine bomber*). He just came down the valley and he landed on his wheels. I couldn't understand how anyone could withstand the hail of lead that was going up. Everybody was shooting at him. Somebody told me that the pilot was shot in the leg – that was the only thing – he's gotta be Blessed, also to come back from that." Some Focke-Wulf fighters followed through the attack with American P-47's coming along behind firing at the German aircraft. The columns couldn't distinguish the difference between the German planes and the American aircraft at low level high speeds – they both had front radial engines, although the P-47 was a much larger plane. The armored columns kept firing at all low flying aircraft. The next time the P-47's came over, they wagged their wings to signal that they were friendly US planes! At this stage of the war, the combat teams were accustomed to roaming Germany without any interference from the Luftwaffe. According to division history, April 2nd was the worst day of air attacks experienced in the war. There were three raids of twenty enemy aircraft and small raids by single aircraft that day.

After the move further east past Weimar and Zeitz, the 6th Armored Division drove to the Mulde River. This river, runs right through the middle of a geographic triangle of three large cities - Leipzig, Chemnitz and Dresden. That's where it halted April 24,1945 upon orders to wait for the Russians, which were not far away. Between that date and the war's end on May 8th, Company B went on many short patrols to round up the German soldiers streaming in to surrender. It was much more healthy for them to surrender to the Americans than the Russians!

The 50th Armored Infantry Battalion set up headquarters in the town of Rochlitz. Ray's squad was outposted in the tiny hamlet of Kleine Milkau (*small milk cow*) – billeted in an old farmhouse. The old lady who lived there did the laundry for the squad in exchange for food rations which the GI's provided. One never saw any German male civilians between the ages of 16 and 60. All those German men were in some type of military organization. Ray was now driving a Jeep for 2nd Lt. Mike Zdrodowski, who had won a Silver Star <u>and</u> a battlefield commission for bravery. One of the jobs was driving an old German doctor around small - close together - villages so he could treat his patients. The doctor had no car nor any way to get gasoline for any vehicle he might find.

One day Ray and his buddy were driving the doctor and a young German lady was walking down the road carrying a tin pail of milk. About a block behind, a freed English prisoner of war, a Sikh complete with turban and long beard, was going down the same road. After the doctor was dropped off, Ray said, " This don't look right, so we turned around and drove back. The Sikh, most likely Indian, had pushed the girl into the ditch and was trying to rape her. Food was precious then. She was struggling to fight him off while still balancing the milk pail without spilling any. We pulled a gun on him and put him on the hood of the Jeep to turn him over to the MP's in the town where the doctor was waiting. We told the MP's what happened and we took some flak. They replied, 'What the hell, she's a German girl and he's an Allied prisoner!' Well, we wouldn't let nothin' like that happen. "

Ray also remembered going to Chemnitz,." I was driving a Jeep and they were taking three or four 2 ½ ton truckloads of displaced persons back to the Russian zone. These were eastern Europeans – Polish or something like that. We was going to turn them over to the Russians in Chemnitz. I'll never forget, we went down the road and just on the outskirts of Chemnitz, the Russians were waiting for us. They had an American Jeep. And, it really looked like it been through the war – a spring was broke, everything on the dash was kicked out. They escorted us. We could only go down one street into Chemnitz to a railroad station. We unloaded them there and went back the same road – they escorted us in and escorted us out." Had the Cold War begun?

The 6th Armored Division moved back from the Mulde River and from headquarters at Apolda beginning on June 15, 1945. July 1st the division moved west again out of what was the Russian zone – later called East Germany until freed from Communist rule in 1989. The Army set up a point scoring system to determine who would go home first. The magic number was 85 points. Any soldier with that number or more would be sent home in the first wave. Each man received points according to his length of service, combat awards, dependents at home, Purple Heart, months of service overseas,etc. A married man with children received 12 points for each child under 18 years of age up to three children. Since the 6th Armored had been designated for demobilization, those veterans with fewer than 85 points were transferred to other divisions going home later or into the Army of Occupation. As a result Company B, 2nd platoon, 1st rifle squad was scattered to the four winds and most of them never saw each other again. What a tragedy - they lost track of each other!

George Hudson Wirth (age 18 on left) & Raymond Frank Mutz (age 20 on right) near Rochlitz, Germany at War's end – May 1945.

Everyone that was eligible for discharge was moving on. The replacements all stayed behind. Ray said, "I was assigned to the 28th Infantry Division (*the same one that marched down the Champs Elysee on August 29, 1944*) but went to LeHavre to Camp Phillip Morris and on to the ship 'Marshall Joffre' . They gave us a physical so you weren't taking any diseases home. We got down to the pier and the 'Marshall Joffre' had to go to England for repairs. I think we waited another week and a half. I was one day out of New York when the Japanese surrendered on August 14, 1945. The soldiers on board were from all over. When we got back to Ft. Meade, Maryland – had all the chow you wanted – all the milk and ice cream you wanted. They processed us in one day. Then I got back on the train to Ft. Logan, Colorado. Right away they give me thirty days leave. After thirty days, I went back to Ft. Logan and they give me another fifteen days. The guy says, 'You're transferred to the 28th Infantry Division which is down in Louisiana. He says,' no sense in you going back down there for two weeks. You'll be eligible for discharge then. I can give you a job here and keep you for two weeks.' " Since he was a wounded veteran, Ray was given a good physical by a Ft. Logan doctor. When the doctor asked Ray how he felt, he replied, "Just fine except for some numbness in my left thigh." The doctor turned him over and without Ray knowing it, pricked the rear of his left thigh. Ray didn't feel a thing waiting for the doctor's diagnosis, " The medic said you have a 10% disability – no, a 20% disability and it's been that way ever since." He was discharged in November 1945.

Like many GI's, when Ray just turned twenty-one years old on October 3,1945, he married his hometown school girlfriend on his first furlough. Ray said, " I went to work for CF&I (Colorado Fuel & Iron). Of course, I had the GI Bill and at that time Pueblo just had a junior college, so I went to school for two years while I worked in the mill. Our first child, Dave, was born in the summer of 1946 and our second son, Rick came along in 1949." Ray spent a life career working for CF&I in the metallurgy department and he really enjoyed his work, especially the people there. In 1972 his 27-year marriage went awry and he stayed single for another 12 years until he married his present wife, Pat, in 1984.

Ray discussed his experience as a soldier in World War II, " When I left to go overseas, I just sort of put home out of my mind. I didn't think there was ever going to be a home – I thought this is going to be a way of life from now on. I didn't ever contemplate about coming home. The only time I thought about coming home was the last two weeks of the war. I was a little flaky then (*and he laughs*). Then in a serious mood he said, " And, some of them didn't make it home in the last two weeks." He reflected back on his wartime experiences, " I can't describe it in the right words. I thought it was a one in a million experience. It was so fantastic in all aspects, the good and the bad. You had some terrible times but you had companionships that were unbelievable - indescribable. You're close to family, your own family, but yet there's a different type of closeness that you have with your fellow soldiers. Boy, what an experience! I wouldn't want to go through it again, I know for sure…it would be impossible to survive again. The really sad part is that I had the opportunity to come back and see a lot more of life, while I had some good friends that I never would get to see again. I think of Sgt. Irwin a lot."

Ray had saved many photographs of his rifle squad and others from the 2nd platoon of Company B, 50th Armored Infantry Battalion, 6th Armored Division. These photos will show what the troops looked like on May 8, 1945 - the end of World War II. The 6th Armored Division was almost exactly 100 miles south of Berlin near the Czechoslovakian border. The major German cities of Dresden, Leipzig and Chemnitz form a triangle. The town of Rochlitz is located in the center of this triangle – 25-45 miles from each of the cities. These pictures were taken nearby by Ray. That's why he is not in any of them.

First Rifle Squad of the 2nd Platoon, Company B. Oakie Morris with Red Cross helmet. 2nd row, from left 1? 2.Sgt.John Gettel, Hagerstown ,Maryland. 3. ? 4. George Petrash, Cleveland, Ohio
3rd row. 1.Charles Strange,St. Louis, Missouri 2. Felix Jezak,

Milwaukee, Wisconsin 3.Robert Lenihan, Lockport, New York.4. Lloyd Moore, Orofino, Idaho.5. George Wirth, Wausau, Wisconsin.5. Matthew Peterson, Plainfield, New Jersey. Note. Halftrack # 47 in background with a 50 caliber machine gun.

Top row from left: 1. George Wirth, Wausau, Wisconsin 2. Carl Scott, St.Louis, Missouri3. Noble Payne, Muscatine, Iowa.

Bottom row: George Petrash, Cleveland, Ohio 2. John Gettel, Hagerstown, Maryland 3. Oakie Morris, New Martinsville, West Virginia 4. Peter Yaniw, Youngstown, Ohio.

From Left: 1. George Graunke, Portage, Wisconsin 2. George Petrash, Cleveland, Ohio 3. Dean Adams,Telford, Tennessee.

89

Ray Mutz's tent mate and buddy at Rochlitz, George Hudson Wirth

From left: Matthew Peterson and Lloyd Moore at our outpost road block. The half track looks like a gypsy wagon.

2nd Lt. Mike Zdrodowski in front of a German Me 109 (Messerschmidt) fighter plane. He won a battlefield commission and a Silver Star. On the right, trying to make post parade soldiers out of combat veterans in June 1945 in Rochlitz, Germany.

George Hudson Wirth and Raymond Frank Mutz meeting for the first time in Nov.1999 at Pueblo, CO since June 1945 in Rochlitz Germany.

PETER P. BETCHNER JR.

Peter and I were in the same rifle squad of Co. "B", 50th Armored Infantry Battalion in the 6th Armored Division, so I know first hand about his experiences. We were rarely at full strength due to casualties, injuries, illness, etc. Our home away from home was half-track # 47. Part of the time we fought as regular infantry and at other times when our armored columns broke through the German lines, we rode in our half-track. When our armored column came under enemy fire, we jumped over the side and into battle.

What few personal belongings we had were carried in a musette bag on a hook in the half-track. One of my personal belongings was a very small address book. In it I had written the names and addresses of most of our squad members – at least the ones I knew from January 1945-to- May 1945 when the war ended. I rediscovered that small address book not long ago.

I didn't really know much about Peter's life prior to the army or what happened to him after his service years until I made contact with him in November 1999. After I became somewhat computer literate, I decided to attempt to locate some of my old Army buddies via the Internet.

Using a search engine on the Internet, I located 6 Betchners in Wisconsin – one was Peter Betchner – not in Milwaukee as listed in my address book – but in Waupaca, Wisconsin. I phoned this Peter Betchner, lo and behold it was my friend. The last time I had any contact with him was on April 13, 1945 in Zeitz, Germany. I made arrangements to visit him soon– some 180 miles distant- for a reunion.

My wife, Chris, and I drove to Waupaca and met Peter and his lovely wife, Helma, at their home. As soon as he opened his door I recognized him immediately – 54 years later. The last time we saw each other, he was 26 years old and I was eighteen.

We enjoyed lunch together and spent the whole afternoon reminiscing about our war experiences. He graciously allowed me to tape our conversations so that I could tell Peter's story. Since that first reunion, we have stopped by many times to visit with Peter and Helma.

His father, Peter Paul Betchner met his wife Catherine Kuth in Germany. She had a previous marriage and had three children from it. So, the young Peter and his bride immigrated to the USA. His father was a migrant farm worker in Europe and learned to speak several languages besides German. His mother died at age 52 when Peter was eleven years old – in 1930 during the Great Depression. She had never learned to speak English. Things were tough for poor immigrant farm families then. Being farmers, there was food on the table, but no money to be made by farming. The Betchners had six children, three boys and three girls of their own, plus three girls from Catherine's previous marriage. Peter was born March 31, 1919 in Cudahy, Wisconsin. He was the second youngest in the family and became a Jr. carrying the same name as his father. The family moved to a farm near Ingalls, Michigan when he was just a tot. His brothers also served in World War II – one in the Air Corps and the other in the Army In a field artillery unit.

Peter attended a one-room schoolhouse for his education. When he graduated from the eighth grade, Peter said, "My father asked me if I wanted to go to high school. I told him no, since we can't pay the taxes on the farm, I'll stay home and help." In 1934 at age 15, he went to work on a neighbor's farm for $3.50 per week including room and board. He worked through the hot summer months. In the wintertime, things were so bad his farm neighbors said, "You can stay here if you want, but we can't pay you." So, he stayed with them for his food and a place to sleep. "One winter I went out to see my Uncle in Pennsylvania and I stayed there 'til February", Peter said. In the Spring his Uncle wrote, "'Do you want to come back and work for me?" Peter answered, "I'd like to but, I don't have any money out here." His Uncle sent him the bus fare.

.   He was sixteen years old in 1935 – the heart of the Great Depression. The employment outlook for a decent job was almost non-existent. He decided to join the CCC's – the Civilian Conservation Corps – which was created in the mid-1930's during President Franklin D. Roosevelt's New Deal administration as an emergency measure.

93

Peter in front of his CCC barracks building, at age seventeen 1936.

The CCC'S offered young men an opportunity to work full time in a quasi military camp atmosphere commanded by a regular Army officer. Peter lied about his age and enrolled at age sixteen on November 14, 1935. The men stayed in army barracks (the same type used a few years later in World War II), wore uniforms and got three square meals a day. In addition, they were paid $30 dollars per month and were expected to send $25 dollars home to their allottee (family). His father kept $15 and sent $10 back to Peter. One of the other Betchner boys was also in the CCC's. He sent money home too. Peter said his father was able to buy a used Plymouth car with the money the two boys sent home. They couldn't afford a car before the family received this extra $30 per month.

Many of the wonderful improvements to our park systems were built by the CCC's and are enjoyed by us today. It was hard outdoor work. The program also disciplined young men and trained them for a military environment. Almost all CCC's served in the Armed Forces in World War II, which soon exploded in September 1939, when Hitler's Nazi regime invaded Poland. They were among the first draftees and volunteers.

Peter said he enjoyed his two hitches in the CCC's. The first enlistment lasted from November 14,1935 until March 31, 1936 and then he went back home to work on his neighbors farm for the summer in Michigan. On March 15, 1937 he enrolled for a one year hitch. The family needed money and jobs were next to impossible to get. One of his jobs was cleaning and servicing CCC vehicles. The garage he worked in was not very wide and most of the drivers had difficulty backing their vehicles into the narrow door openings. So they asked the young eighteen year old kid to do it for them – and he loved to show off his skills. Toward the end of his last term – in 1938 – Peter told his Captain that he was going to join the regular American peacetime Army. The Captain tried to talk him out of his decision to no avail. On September 30, 1938, Peter was discharged from the CCC's. I asked him about his time in the CCC's. He said, "It was a good thing for us and most were darned good kids! It was like a soldiers camp and we didn't have any discipline problems. I followed orders and did my job just like the others!"

He enlisted in the peacetime U.S. Army on October 11, 1938, eleven days after being discharged from the CCC's. Peter spent two years of his three year Army enlistment term in the Panama Canal Zone as it was called in those days. He remembers the Army saying, " If you served in Panama, you'll never go to Hell because

you've already served your hitch there." He tells about the awful heat of Panama in Army uniforms. These soldiers manned big guns and emplacements protecting the canal. In his last year he was transferred back to Ft. Lee, Virginia where he was part of the Cadre as a recruit instructor. In October 1941 he was discharged with the rank of Sergeant– about two months before Pearl Harbor.

Peter Betchner during his first hitch in the Army

By early 1941 the USA was starting to gear up for war, although at a snails pace. Peter got a job at the Chain Belt Company in Milwaukee. He became a machinist working on a slotting machine making breech-blocks for the US Army's 155 millimeter artillery pieces. The 155's were called "Long Toms" by GI's. Breech-blocks are the loading apparatus, which must be opened to eject a shell and closed when sliding in a new shell. When war in the United States broke out, December 7, 1991 – Pearl Harbor Day --, Peter had already served three years in the Army. His time in the CCC's also counted toward his military service. He was now working hard in the defense industry and because of this, he had a low draft status at the beginning of the war.

In 1944, after D-Day on June 6th, the Army realized their casualties were greater than expected. The Selective Service Administration increased their draft quotas and Peter was called up on July 19th. At the induction center in Milwaukee, new draftees were lined up. A Non-Com (non- commissioned officer) would go down the line and every fourth man would be designated for the Navy. Naturally, when he got to Peter he said, "Navy". Peter replied, " I've already spent three years in the Army. I'm not going into the Navy! I'm an Army man". He was inducted into the Army at Ft. Sheridan, Illinois. His military papers show he was 5 feet-6 ½ inches tall and weighed 133 pounds. Peter was a small wiry guy. His Army serial number was 6-945-559, the same one assigned to him back in 1938. Once you enter the Army, you always keep the same number.

Basic training was at Camp Hood, Texas – one of the largest IRTC centers (Infantry Replacement Training Center) in the military. The former Sergeant was now a Private. After getting toughened up again, Peter started overseas on January 1, 1945 - Happy New Year!- boarding the Queen Mary luxury liner that had been converted to a troop carrier. The Queen carried upwards of ten thousand fresh replacement troops in an unescorted dash across the North Atlantic. At this stage of the war, troop ships were safer from U-boats by going full speed ahead rather than traveling in a slow convoy. Besides, the Army needed infantry replacements right now. Peter arrived in Scotland early on January 7th. Like so many young American soldiers of German heritage, Peter was about to do battle with the country where both his mother and father were born and grew up.

After a train ride to Southampton and a ride across the English Channel in a LSI (Landing Ship Infantry) he disembarked in LeHavre, France at the American Army staging camps. They were named after the most popular cigarettes in fashion at that time – Camps, Lucky Strike, Chesterfield and Philip Morris. From there he boarded a "Forty & Eight" French railroad boxcar – so named after use in World War I because they held forty men or eight horses. Most American Legion posts carry this name. He was sent to a "Reppo Deppo" (replacement depot) – in Reims, France, where Peter was assigned to the 6th Armored Division, 50th Armored Infantry Battalion, Company B. It didn't take long to get these boys to the front, which at that time was in eastern Belgium and Luxembourg. He was a replacement in the Battle of the Bulge.

Two things that were in short supply at the front then were ammunition and infantry replacements. The burn rate of ammunition at the rate of use was about 21 days. Secretary of War, Henry Stimson, scrounged US Army installations for ammo and cut infantry training cycles short by two weeks to speed up the flow of men. On January 7th 1945, General Eisenhower sent a message to Gen. George Marshall's Combined Chiefs of Staff to keep up the flow of replacements. He asked for expedited shipments of critical ammunition types and tires. By middle to late February 1945, US Armies were near proper supplies and manpower. The replacements had arrived!

. I first met Peter Betchner in late January 1945 in the tiny hamlet of Kalborn, Luxembourg which is on the north end of this tiny Duchy. I had gone overseas on January 6, 1945 on the Ile de France, former luxury liner, five days after Peter. We were stacked in bunks five men high making it to Grenoc, Scotland at full speed in just over four days. We had only two meals per day – too many soldiers on board to feed them three times. The rough winter north Atlantic seas caused the ship to lift and plunge into the seas. The propeller came completely out of the water and accelerated its spin before its next plunge into the sea. Seasickness kept the chow lines in check. We also took our watch turns on guard duty - watching for U-boats.

Kalborn, Luxembourg is just a few hundred yards from the "Skyline Drive" as the road was called by GI's. It was so named because one could stand on this high ridge road, look to the east and peer directly into Germany about one air mile away. One half mile down a very steep heavily wooded hill was the Our river, which is the border between Luxembourg and Germany. Going up hill on the German side of the border was the Siegfried line or Westwall as known by the Germans. The northern Ardennes region, called the "Schnee Eifel" in German, is the worst terrain in which to fight. The steep hills, almost small mountains, are separated by numerous small river gorges. They run largely north to south while American Armies were headed east. Each forested hill and river was a problem!

Not many vehicles dallied along the Skyline Drive as they made target practice for the deadly German 88 mm artillery weapons. When we got near the area, Army 2 ½ ton trucks dropped us off and we hiked in to Kalborn. It had about five buildings including one large farm building where several families lived. There was a tiny white church across the farmyard. No civilians occupied the area - the roofs had been blown off the buildings. There was a frozen black horse on the only road in Kalborn and one dead civilian corpse in a sitting position leaning against a farm building. On Dec. 16th 1944, the beginning of the Battle of the Bulge, German SS troops had rounded up seven young men from this Luxembourg hamlet and executed them near the tiny church. In 1995 we visited with a young woman in Kalborn, Marie-Paul Schmitz Peiffer, who told this story.

Our rifle squad was quartered in one room of the farmhouse the first night. An Army blanket hung on both sides of the door to keep out any flicker of the two candles that were lit. Light would bring in artillery fire. There I introduced myself to Peter who was 25 years old. Since I was eighteen, I thought he must have been in the squad a long time being that old. I didn't realize most of the men were replacements for the original soldiers who started out in Normandy in the breakout on July 28th, 1944.

Other men of our squad were: Dean Adams from Telford, Tennessee a tall lanky squirrel hunter from one of those "hollers" – a wonderful friend who didn't have much education but was very intelligent. He saved us many times with his hunter's instinct. Then there was Lloyd Moore from Orofino, Idaho. He had been through a lot and was a nervous smoking type. John Gettel from Maryland was our Sgt. and a good one! Okey Morris (how about that name?) was our half-track # 47 driver from West Virginia. He was the squad comedian. There is a photo of him at wars end wearing a German hat, holding a finger under his nose and doing a "Heil Hitler" pose near our half-track. Two were from Ohio, George Petrash – Cleveland and Peter Yaniw from Youngstown. Matthew Peterson came from Plainfield, New Jersey and Robert Lenihan – Lockport, New York. John Axelson from Milaca, Minnesota. So you see, we had a mix of soldiers in our squad - from all over the USA – all were replacements except Okey.

Why were there so many replacements? The 50th Armored Infantry Battalion had a full staff complement of 1,000 men. During the battle period from July 28th,1944 (the St. Lo, Normandy breakout) to May 8th, 1945 (the war's end in eastern Germany near Rochlitz on the Mulde River) the Battalion had 1,045 battle casualties. There were 213 soldiers killed in action (KIA), 829 wounded in action (WIA) and 3 missing in action (MIA) In addition there were 859 non-battle casualties, which were men evacuated from the division area. These statistics were not unusual for a combat infantry unit. This meant that the 50th AIB needed 1,904 replacements during this nine month period.

After the Battle of the Bulge, both armies were exhausted from the fighting. It was the largest land battle ever fought by the United States Army – somewhere around 500,000 men participated by the end and German estimates run from 250, 000 to 400,000 during the campaign. It started with a surprise attack on the thinly held American lines at dawn on December 16,1944 and ended on January 27th 1945, at which time the Germans were pushed back into Germany and into the Siegfried line. It was fought during the cold winter months – the coldest winter recorded in the last 100 years. Hitler planned the attack under the greatest secrecy and caught top American Generals and their Intelligence staffs completely by surprise. Many excellent books have been written by historians describing this awesome struggle – when the Germans were considered to be almost finished.

Kalborn is about 30 km or 19 air miles east of Bastogne, Belgium. By road, through the twisting valleys and rivers of the Ardennes, it is twice as far. This area was originally defended by the 110th Infantry Regiment of the 28th Infantry Division. They fought valiantly for three days against overwhelming numbers of the enemy (ten to one). The Germans didn't overrun Clervaux, the 110th Regimental Headquarters, until December 18th thereby giving the 101st Airborne Div. enough time to get to Bastogne for their heroic stand there.

Peter's 50th AIB was assigned the task of crossing the Our river into Germany, to face the Siegfried line, hold the position while maintaining aggressive patrols. To set the scene for his first action, I am quoting from an earlier book that I wrote.

Peter was about to get his first glimpse of Germany. " The squad arose early on a cold snowy morning well before daybreak in early February in the hamlet of Kalborn, to start forward to relieve troops on the front line. This winter had been one of the coldest on record in Europe.

The squad had a quick breakfast including hot coffee prepared by our company cooks. Checking our gear and ammunition was critical. We carried a full pack which included a blanket roll, shelter half (one-half of a pup tent), a change of olive drab underwear and socks. Nothing white was allowed in a combat unit for fear a flash of white might give away a position. We also had a few personal items such as a small wallet, a few snapshots from home, shaving items and a toothbrush. At this point, all worldly possessions were carried on your back."

Peter was armed with an M-1 Garrand semi-automatic rifle, full cartridge belt, two extra bandoliers of 30 calibre ammunition slung over his shoulders and across his chest, a bayonet and two hand grenades clipped loosely to metal rings on his back pack straps.

Clothing consisted of lined pants, wool shirts, field jackets (overcoats were too clumsy, as they were awkward when running), gloves and wool socks. Our boots were called arctic packs. These were all rubber feet and leather tops including felt linings. They must have been copied from the footwear dairy farmers in Wisconsin wore around barnyards in the winter months. They were quite warm when dry – but the danger was sweating feet – no way for the moisture to escape through the rubber. Wet feet were terribly cold – especially at night in the foxholes. If you didn't change socks when your feet got wet, they turned to a spongy white color and cracked open under the toes. This caused swelling and bleeding (trenchfoot), often severe enough to warrant a trip to the division hospital and sometimes requiring amputation of toes.

His pack, rifle, ammunition, helmet etc. weighed about 60 pounds. This is what he lugged with him. A good thing he had rugged basic training at Camp Hood, Texas. That's a lot of weight to carry on a 133 pound frame!.

It is important to remember that World War II was not trench warfare as was World War I in 1914-1918. It was basically fought on the rifle squad level (8-12 men) or the platoon level (30-50 men). Often members of the same company (200 men) didn't know each other. In the Kalborn Our river border area, (between Luxembourg and Germany) the American and German armies were stuck in a static position from January 28 until February 20,1945.

Our 6th Armored Division occupied a sector 20,000 yards long or approximately 11 ½ miles with two battalions of armored infantry on the line and one battalion in reserve. Each battalion had about 1,000 men, so you can see that only small groups of soldiers could occupy this extensive distance – plenty of chance for enemy infiltration.

Just what was the Siegfried line that Peter was facing with his squad? It was a defensive line of 350 miles constructed over a period of years from the mid-1930's to 1940. It extended from Holland down the western frontier of Germany to the border of France and Switzerland. It was supposed to be impenetrable. Concrete pillboxes and bunkers were built to take maximum advantage of fields of fire. Some were as much as three stories deep where soldiers slept off duty and ammunition was stored. They were further protected by anti-tank obstacles as well as mine fields and barbed wire entanglements. Often they were interconnected by trenches dug near small hamlets so German troops could move to the town or out of it without being observed or exposed to enemy fire. This was Hitler's Westwall.

Peter's first attack against enemy positions took place on February 20,1945. The slim bridgehead into Germany, held east of the Our river, was perhaps a few hundred yards – certainly less than one mile deep. General Patton wanted to get things moving and he surely wanted to start before Gen. Montgomery's 21st Army Group further north. Patton never agreed with Monty's more deliberate planning and movement strategy.

Oral orders for the attack were issued by the 6th Armored Division Commander, Major General Robert W. Grow. February 19th military documents state, "By taking advantage of the bridgehead held by CCB (Combat Command B), an assault could be made against the Siegfried Line defense without the necessity of forcing a crossing of the Our river in the face of pillboxes that lined its banks from Dasburg to the south. The plan called for an initial easterly penetration by CCB and an envelopment from the north pushing south behind the pillboxes to cut off retreat of the Germans. Troops were positioned for the attack, as enemy artillery and mortar fire increased. Final instructions were given the soldiers."

CCB was organized into three main attacking teams supported by anti-aircraft, mechanized cavalry, reconnaissance, three field artillery battalions and VIII Corps artillery reinforcing the firepower for the initial assault. Corps artillery was composed mainly of 155-mm cannons (Long Toms) that were usually fired from a distance of five miles or more behind the lines. The shell diameter was 6.10 inches and it packed a terrific wallop upon detonation.

Peter's squad was part of CT 50 (Combat Team 50), commanded by Lt. Col. Albert N. Ward Jr., which was composed of:

The 50th Armored Infantry Battalion ------------------1000 men.

Company C 68th Tank Battalion-----------------------20 medium tanks

1 platoon CO A 603rd Tank Destroyer Battalion ---3 TD's

1 platoon CO B 25th Armd. Engineer Battalion------40 men

CT 50 infiltrated units through the hamlet of Kalborn and across the bridge to the reverse slope in front of the pillboxes during the night.

February 20th - at 0645 hour, artillery laid an intensive preparation over the entire front for twenty minutes, then lifted for ten minutes to allow the enemy to come out of their pillboxes and man their defenses to meet the probable attack. Then for one minute all artillery concentrated on the small target area of the first objective with a terrific TOT (Time On Target) by every available artillery piece including all Corps artillery in this sector. This was the signal for the attack. In the meantime CCA made a diversionary movement on the south flank supported by a smoke generating company and fire which attracted much of the enemy artillery and mortar reaction. So states the official record.

CT 50 moved to attack at 0715 hours to face expected awesome fire from the pillboxes. The plan was executed perfectly since enemy fire was comparatively light. Initial gains against the Siegfried Line were two miles in depth and two miles in width. A total of 40 pillboxes were taken with a loss of only two soldiers killed among the other wounded. The first pillbox was seized at 0830 hours. One pillbox held out all day and night and was finally taken on February 21st when 450 pounds of TNT were placed against the steel door and detonated. One German officer and eleven enlisted men were dragged out in a stunned condition.

CT 50 continued to attack each day from tiny hamlet to hamlet, across muddy fields, through woods and crossing small streams. Ground was gained and resistance by the Germans became sporadic but heavy at times. By February 27th the Combat Team was at the banks of the small Prum River near Lunebach, some 15 km (about 9 miles) east from the Our river starting point. At the Prum River, the 50th AIB ran into a hornet's nest.

The official record of the action," ...our troops reached Lunebach, where combat patrols from " C ' Company probed the defenses of that town without meeting the heavy

opposition that was expected. In light of the week just passed, there was no reason to believe this town would present any great difficulty, yet Lunebach was to become a village of death. The severest casualties came from cunningly concealed booby traps, which in turn attracted a terrific enemy artillery barrage. Despite heavy losses and fanatic opposition, our troops cleared Lunebach and the immediate vicinity in a drive that carried Task Force Ward across the cold icy Prum River. The last two days of February were marked by a continuous hail of fire poured into our positions, which eventually forced our withdrawal to the original lines west of the Prum. The set-back was merely temporary however, and at dawn on the last day of February the Task Force mounted a second attack that brought it across the Prum, this time to stay."

(OPPOSITE, TOP) Lunebach, Germany, 1945, after the U.S. Army had fought through the town. Not only was every large city burned out, but thousands of German villages and hamlets like this were wrecked by the Allied armies. (Army—OWI)

Lunebach, Germany at the tiny Prum river ~ May 1995

Lunebach, Germany in

1945 and 1995

The Army photograph of Lunebach is worth a thousand words. Can you imagine what it was like scrambling across the mud and icy stream, - trying to keep your rifle high

103

out of the water - running to the nearest shelter of a building, rock wall or tree?

On March 1st, Peter's company took the small German hamlet of Matzerath at 1605 hour. It took all day from Lunebach to move one and one-half miles east to Matzerath. Near the village some small arms fire erupted. Peter was wounded for the first time in his neck and face by stone chips and bullet fragments. The medics removed the small shrapnel and with some disinfectants and small bandages sent him back to the squad. (Editors note: I have a Nazi banner made of ersatz silk fabric with the black swastika in a white circle enscripted, "seine kameraden von Matzerath" (*your comrades from Matzerath.)*

After two weeks of fighting through the Siegfried Line, the 6th Armored Dv. was replaced by the 90th Infantry Dv. on March 4th. The 6th Armored was assembled near the town of Arzfeld, approximately eight miles to the rear of the front. For the first time since it entered combat on July, 27,1944, the entire division was out of the front lines.

From Coutances, France to Avranches (spearheading the breakthrough south from St. Lo, in Normandy) and the 200 mile race to the Brittany port of Brest; at Lorient; from the Nancy bridgehead to the Siegfried defenses of Saarbrucken; and from Bastogne through the Siegfried Line to Schoenecken on the Nims river, the 6th Armored Dv. had been in continuous action.

All Army combat infantrymen who participated in this attack were promoted to PFC, Private First Class, which meant another $ 10 per month pay bringing it to a total of $85 per month! They also received the Bronze Star.

The division was now being prepared and refitted for its next assignment. Troops got showers and clean uniforms. The Red Cross truck with pretty American girls brought hot coffee and doughnuts to them. The 6th Armored was being transferred to the 7th Army, secretly, in the south of France. Shoulder patches and vehicle markings were removed and radio silence was imposed. The division traveled 165 miles to Vic Sur Seille, France arriving there March 12th.

On March 5th, Ike and Patton flew to Luneville to meet with Gen. Patch, head of the 7th Army. On the way, Eisenhower told Patton, " you are not only good, but lucky and as you know, Napoleon prized luck over skill ". Patch was stuck in the southern sector, between Switzerland and France. Patton's orders were to cross the Moselle River in the north, cut through the Palatinate region behind the Westwall and hurry southeast to the Rhine River. Patch was to break through the Westwall, take Saarbrucken, and slice northeast to the Rhine. This maneuver by Patton's Third Army and Patch's 7th Army would entrap a huge part of the German Army defending the Westwall. The Germans had been given " no retreat " orders by Hitler.

" **The Stars and Stripes"** Army newspaper, Nancy edition on Wednesday, March 21, 1945 printed a front page bulletin:

" 3rd and 7th Link Up

SHAEF- The 6th Armored Div. of the 7th Army and the 26th Inf. Div. of the 3rd Army made contact yesterday about 12 miles west of Kaiserlautern, it was announced early today".

Another short article in the "Stars and Stripes"

"West Front Casualties 34,468 in February

Washington, March 20 – Secretary of War, Henry L. Stimson revealed today that U.S. ground forces casualties on the Western front in February were 34,468, the smallest in three months. Casualties **since D-Day totaled 425,007**.The February total includes 4,145 killed, 26,436 wounded and 3,887 missing. **Overall casualties for all U.S. forces since Dec. 7, 1941, now total 839,589."**

These are staggering numbers. Each and every single one represents some young American sacrificing his body so that future generations might live in a more peaceful world without totalitarianism. These were sobering statistics AND the war was not yet over!

In the meantime, another article on page 7: " Byron Nelson of Toledo shot a four under-par-68 to gain a tie with Sammy Snead at the end of the $10,000 Charlotte Open golf tournament.... First prize money of $2,000 will go to the winner of their 18-hole playoff match today." For many Americans on the Home Front, it was business and play as usual. For those doing the fighting, it was a different story!

The 6th Armored was busy advancing through the hilly rugged Palatinate area of southwestern Germany to the Rhine plain. It crossed the Rhine on March 25th at Oppenheim in a 14-hour parade of bumper to bumper vehicles across a single pontoon bridge. It had now completed its work with the 7th U.S. Army and was reassigned to Gen. Patton's 3rd Army.

The XII Corps of the Third Army had a mission to exploit the bridgehead across the Rhine maintained by the 5th and 90th Infantry Divisions. With the 6th Armored on the left flank   (north) and the 4th Armored on the right, they drove northeast to Frankfurt and then crossed the Main River just east of Frankfurt.

The war after crossing the Rhine went fast for the Armored divisions. Gen. Patton's armor was sent scurrying north to Kassel. The Ruhr pocket was about to collapse after the German Army had been surrounded. Gen. Bradley then directed Patton to hurry his troops east to cut Germany in half and meet the Russians near the Elbe River.

The 6th Armored Div. went east through Muhlhausen and passed just north of Weimar. About 6 miles northwest of Weimar, there in Saxony, ironically where the German Republic was formed after World War I, the 6th Armored stumbled across Buchenwald. This notorious concentration camp had been taken over by the inmates as their Nazi SS guards had fled ahead of the approaching 6th Armored columns. On April 11th, 1945 a patrol of four men from the 9th Armored Inf. Bn. in a Scout Car were guided there by some escaped Russian inmates and discovered the horror of this terrible camp. These were the first American soldiers to enter Buchenwald. Much has been written about Buchenwald. There have been many mistaken claims, by individuals and military units, for the liberation of this camp by heroic fighting action. The hard facts are recorded in our 6th Armored history and supported by meticulous German history scholars today-- there was no battle. The Nazi guards knew Patton's armored columns were closing in on this area and fled. They discarded their uniforms, changed into civilian clothes and attempted to disappear into the nearby woods. Some inmates gathered weapons and hunted down the German guards. Those that were found were shot. Today there are lecturers speaking about their liberation of Buchenwald. These impostors have attempted to twist history for their individual financial benefit.

April 13th, elements of the 6th Armored Dv. were in the city of Zeitz. Company B of the 50th Armored Infantry Battalion moved through the southern part of the town and came upon a German Kaserne – a permanent military station occupied by some 700 soldiers commanded by an SS officer that did not want to surrender. Help from the Air Force was called in by our CombatTeam 50 commander. We marked the building with smoke bombs where the German commander was located. Shortly P 47's – fighter planes with bomb carrying capacity --soon appeared overhead. A bomb was dropped through the roof and that took care of that building.

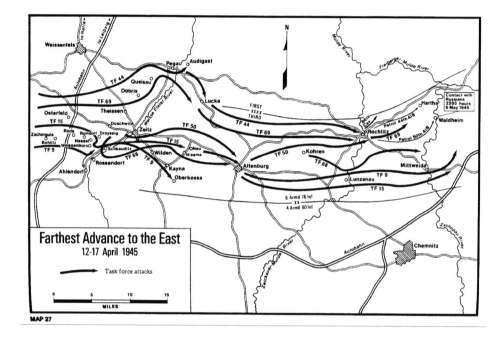

Map courtesy of 6th Armored Assn., George Hoffman's THE SUPER SIXTH 1975

Now the next building in front was to be cleared of the enemy. It was here that Peter was wounded again. His rifle squad was hunkered down behind a small embankment next to a road facing the parade ground in front of a large barracks building. "B" Company was supported by several half-tracks and a tank.

2nd Lt. Ferraro, the platoon leader, gave the orders to commence firing at the windows of the building to give cover to the first men to charge across the open space. Rifle fire from the soldiers and machine gun fire from the half-tracks opened up on the upper stories of the building. Peter and two others ran across the parade ground to the building seeking the shelter of a concrete supply ramp going down to the basement level. Enemy bullets bounced off the concrete. Suddenly Peter spun around and his hands flew up in the air throwing his rifle. He hit the concrete hard, as though someone chopped his feet from out under him. His helmet flew off. A bullet entered his left groin traveled through his body exiting out his right buttocks. He lay still. His face looked green. His buddies thought he was dead, he didn't respond.

They yelled for a Medic. Peter later said, "It didn't hurt bad." Then added, " But in the front, it felt like someone was in there tearing me apart." Asked what went through his mind, he replied, " I wasn't worried about dying. But, I didn't know how bad I was hurt. I worried about being crippled for life. I played like I was dead because I knew if I moved they *(the Germans)* would put another bullet in me."

One of his buddies pulled him down the ramp by his feet to get him out of the line of fire. A half-track backed down near the building with a driver and Medic to treat Peter. Normally the wounded would be carried out by a litter or a Jeep with litters on it. It was safer for an armored half-track to do the rescue work. Okey Morris backed half-track # 47 down toward the concrete ramp. When he got out, he was wearing a Red Cross helmet which had been given to him by our medic to use when he picked up wounded. As he bent down to assist the medic helping Peter, a shot rang out and Oakie got a bullet through the top of his Red Cross helmet and was not scratched. He was proud of that helmet, carrying it in the half-track to the end of the war. There is a photo of our rifle squad in Rochlitz Germany with Okey lying on the ground wearing his Red Cross helmet. *(Ray Mutz Chapter)*

The other two soldiers went about their work. They opened the steel door to the basement, tossed two hand grenades in and then jumped inside each firing a rifle clip of 9 bullets into the hallway. Other members of Peter's squad joined these two soldiers and cleared the building with about 120 Germans surrendering. This was near the end of the war. They knew they were beaten but feared being shot by their own SS officers if they surrendered. As they ran from the building some were fired upon by the SS.

Peter said, "As the medic was working on me, a bullet hit the upper part of his Red Cross helmet, penetrated the steel, ricocheted out but didn't touch his scalp" The Medic cut his pants to the wounds, put sulfa powder on them and then bandaged as best as possible. He also received the standard shot of morphine to control pain. The half-track took him into the center of Zeitz to an Aid Station. He was placed on a kitchen table where he was further treated. Soon a few enemy artillery shells whistled in and Peter recalls they hit the floor while he was lying on top of the table.

From there he was transported to the Division hospital and stayed overnight. On the evening of April 13th, he remembers hearing about the death of President Roosevelt on April 12, 1945. The next morning, April 14th, he was flown by a twin engine C-47 Hospital plane to LeMans, France for more operations. The pilot told the wounded that he would be flying close to the ground, at low level, so a stray German plane could not shoot at them from underneath. He apologized for the bumpy ride. Army doctors could not believe how the bullet could go clear through his body, from the left groin coming out his right buttocks without hitting a major artery or organ. Peter recovered from his surgeries in two months. He was one lucky soldier to have survived!

About his recovery during the summer of 1945 in LeMans, Peter said, "I enjoyed the city. There were outdoor cafes, good food, music and friendly people." He was still not sent home even though the war had ended. He described his Army duty," I drove a Jeep – chauffeured an officer around."

Peter's date of departure from Europe was November 27,1945.He was shipped home to the USA aboard a Liberty ship. The trip was slow (Liberty ships traveled about 10-15 knots) and of course the seas were rough during the winter months. He arrived home passing the Statue of Liberty in New York harbor on December 9th. After taking a train to Ft. Sheridan, Illinois, along the north shore of Chicago, he was discharged on December 15, 1945 – just in time to be home before Christmas.

We chatted about his disability. Peter said, " For quite a few years I could hardly shovel snow or do things like that." The Army awarded him 50% disability pay as a wounded veteran. His original payments were $50 dollars per month. His wife, Helma spoke up, " Back then that was a lot of money. We laugh about that now!"

I asked Helma what she remembers about the World War II years. She said," Our family (of six children) didn't have a car. We went everywhere on public transportation – buses, trolleys and trains. I was a telephone operator working at American Telegraph and Telephone in Shorewood, a suburb of Milwaukee. On Sunday afternoons, the AT&T

employees would sponsor USO parties for Servicemen in the Milwaukee area. We rented the American Legion Hall for $10 and we all brought something to eat – cakes, cookies etc. Then we'd have music for dancing."

Peter returned home to Milwaukee. He got a job in a furniture store. He learned the business and later had his own furniture store. In the Fall of 1949 he met Helma Abler at a dancehall, The Roof, on Wisconsin Ave. They married May 20, 1950 and celebrated their Golden Wedding anniversary in the year 2000.They have a family of four children –three boys and a girl. Their daughter lives in Lafayette, Colorado. Their sons live not far from Waupaca, Wisconsin, a nice small town, where Peter and Helma decided to retire in 1982. They live in a new small 1st floor condominium which suits them just fine – needing a minimum of care.

Down the road about one mile is the Wisconsin Veterans Home in the town of King. It is a beautiful lakeside setting for such a wonderful facility - where all veterans and their and their families can retire to, if need be. It was started after the Civil War when many wounded veterans were indigent and could not support themselves. The historic white frame cottages built in the late eighteen hundreds are now being renovated to add to the charm of the Home.

Peter Betchner (age 81) and George H. Wirth (age 74) June 2000

It was my honor and privilege to get reacquainted with Peter after 54 and one-half years since we were in the same rifle squad and traveled Europe in half-track # 47 together from January 1945 to April14th, 1945. I happen to know his story very well, since I was the eighteen-year-old soldier who was standing alongside him on the concrete ramp in Zeitz when he was wounded and pulled him down the ramp out of the line of fire.

JOHN HOWARD AXELSON

John was born in McGregor, North Dakota on April 2,1925. He was the first baby born into the Swedish family of Enoch Axelson. His father was born in Varmland, Sweden in 1891. Enoch immigrated to the USA at age 17, in 1908, as a teen-ager to escape the military there, before World War I broke out in 1914. However, he was drafted into the American Army in World War I and served in Europe. After the war he did get to visit his family in Sweden. He returned to the USA living in South Chicago, Illinois for a short time before going to Larimore, No. Dakota to work during the wheat harvest at his Aunt's farm.

John's mother, Esther Nelson, was born in 1891 in Nelson County, North Dakota in a sod shanty built by her father. She was the oldest of 11 children – at home in the prairies of North Dakota. Esther worked in a cooks car – cooking and baking for harvest crews – often in summer kitchen temperatures of 120 degrees. Esther and Enoch met there and married in 1922 in Moorhead, Minnesota. For a while they farmed in McGregor, No. Dakota, then moved to Duluth in 1925 after their son was born. Enoch got a job in a steel mill. Their second child, a little girl Eva, came along in 1930 – born in the first year of the Great Depression. In 1933 the family moved to a farm in Milaca, Minnesota, about 50 miles north of Minneapolis.

John grew up in Milaca where he attended a rural school and spoke only Swedish. His sister said he loved school, never missed a day, was well liked and had many friends. A big strong farm boy, he played football at Milaca High School graduating in June 1943. On July 21, 1944 he was inducted into the Army three and one half months after his 19th birthday.

At this stage of the war in Europe, after D-Day on June 6th and before the Allied breakout at St. Lo in Normandy on July 25th, casualty rates among American soldiers were much higher than expected. The Army needed young replacements quickly. John was sent to Camp Hood, Texas for his basic Infantry training. The usual combat training period included 17 weeks of basic training and then a two-week furlough home before reassignment – which at this time meant heading overseas to Europe. His training cycle ended just about the time the Battle of the Bulge broke out on December 16, 1944. Before going overseas, he got a furlough. At home in Milaca, his mother said, "John, you should save your money for a rainy day!" John answered, " These are my rainy days!" He was rushed to the east coast and on December 28th embarked for Europe.

This was a tough time for parents to see their teenage soldiers going into battle overseas. While the US Government tried to play down casualties, the people back home could read the lists in their local papers. It was becoming apparent that World War II had become the worst war for Americans. American soldiers suffered 1,079,162 casualties in World War II followed by the second worst – the Civil War with 646,392. Third was World War I with 320,710 and then the Vietnam War, 211,556 and the Korean War, 140,200.

In November 1944 General Bull, G-2 on General Eisenhower's staff, was sent hurrying to Washington, D.C. to plead with Secretary of War, Henry Stimson, for more infantry replacements. The war had slowed down with the Germans behind the Siegfried line and Americans battling under severe weather conditions in November in the Hurtgen forests – an ideal setting for defense, but a terrible hilly area for the attackers. The American General staffs were determined to force their way through this area and decimated both the US 4th Infantry Division and the 28th Inf. Dv.- divisions which again in December were hit by the Germans in the Battle of the Bulge. Gen. Patton had his Third Army pounding away at the Germans south of Luxembourg near the French city of Metz with limited success and high losses. So, the 6th Armored Division needed replacements, especially in the three Infantry Battalions. John Axelson was headed there.

The naval war in the Atlantic was won at this date by the US Navy and the Air Corp. While there was still danger from some German U-Boats, the majority had been sunk. The overwhelming shipment of supplies, from the United States in convoys, were still pouring into England. In order to move troops quickly to Europe in the safest manner, all of the large pre-war luxury liners of the British, Americans and the French were converted into troop ships. They included the Queen Mary, the United States and the Normandie – all could squeeze in about ten thousand soldiers stacked in bunks five high. They were high-speed ships which could travel at 30 knots far beyond the speed of U-boats and move from the east coast ports of New York and Boston to Scotland in four days. Of course, the General High Staff nightmare was a sinking of a troop ship in the North Atlantic in winter. The only possible sinking would have taken place if one of the liners had passed through a U-boat Wolfpack or there was an engine failure. Every soldier on board had this possibility in the back of his mind.

A large military band would pipe the replacements up the gangplank. A favorite tune of the time, "Don't Fence Me In", was played frequently - to the groan of the GI'S marching up the ramp. Red Cross ladies passed out little cloth bags to each soldier – usually containing writing paper, pencil, toothpaste and other small toilet items. The GI'S would be fully loaded with new combat gear, their helmets and rifles but no ammunition. Once these big liners slipped out of the harbors in the night, at full speed ahead, they traveled with lights out. Each soldier had his life jacket and the first morning at sea there was a life drill. It must have been a moral booster because jumping into the North Atlantic with a life vest in the winter was certain death. Soldiers had their duties including two hour watches for submarines on the deck – without binoculars. There were so many troops crammed into the ship, the Navy could only serve two meals per day. It didn't matter that much because most of the men were sea sick at one time or another. The bunk room floors were usually coated with vomit. Some soldiers turned green and didn't eat for four days. North Atlantic waters in the winter are rough and stormy. These giant ships going full speed would toss up out of the water, the propellers would spin faster and then the hull would pound down into the next wave – some of which could be thirty feet high. When the ships got within air range of England, they usually had air cover and destroyers to escort them. Most of the big ships landed at Grenoc, Scotland and the GI's were a happy lot to disembark – even if they were going to war!

It so happened that three members of the same 1st rifle squad, 2nd platoon, Company B, 50th Armored Infantry Battalion, 6th Armored Division, embarked for Europe within ten days of each other. John Axelson left on December 28, 1944, Peter Betchner on January 1, 1945 and I left on the Ile de France on January 7, 1945. We all joined the squad as infantry replacements. Both John and Peter trained at Camp Hood, Texas and I trained at Camp Fannin near Tyler, Texas.

From Scotland we took trains south to Army camps in the Portsmouth, England area on the coast of the English Channel. As soon as the military could organize a shipload, we boarded smaller vessels to cross the 100 mile distance to LeHavre – about a five hour voyage. The French harbor of LeHavre, where the Seine River empties into the English Channel, was scattered with debris and some sunken ships. GI's, with full battle gear including rifles, had to disembark by climbing down a net over the side to a smaller vessel – usually a Higgins boat which carried about thirty soldiers for the short trip to the dock. From there we all went through one of the three Army camps named after the popular cigarettes of the day, Lucky Strike, Chesterfield or Phillip Morris. This was before the times when we learned how deadly tobacco was for our health. Every PX was loaded with cigarettes at cheap prices for soldiers - $.50 per carton. Our K-ration meal boxes (about the size of a Cracker Jack box) even had a small box inside with three cigarettes.

John, Peter Betchner and I joined the same rifle squad within a few days of each other in late January 1945. Company B, 50th Armored Infantry Battalion was billeted in the tiny hamlet of Kalborn in the very northern part of Luxembourg in a farm house with part of the barn roof blown off. It was good shelter from the cold. Since John was a new big young strong soldier, our second Lieutenant platoon leader, William N. Ferraro, gave him the job of BAR (Browning automatic rifle) man. The BAR, a light machine gun, was a left over from World War I. It weighed about 22 pounds and could fire 30 caliber bullets at the rate of 500 rounds per minute from a cartridge clip, which held 20 shells. I was designated as John's ammunition carrier. My job was to carry two steel ammo boxes as well as my own rifle and ammunition. John had some training with a BAR. He could take it apart and clean it. I had to learn on the job as I had never fired a BAR. The BAR was notorious for jamming if it got dirty. It also had a small bipod, which fitted onto the end of the barrel for stability. The BAR assignment was not relished. We were told to fire only short bursts – three to five shells at a time and then move if possible. Muzzle flashes could give away a location to the enemy!

Lt. Ferraro, was a feisty small Italian boy from Bloomfield, New Jersey. He was probably in his early twenties, but seemed older to me since I was eighteen. I remember the first thing he told me when I joined the squad. He pointed his finger at me and said, " Wirth, if you don't pay attention to me, you won't last three days!" But, when you're eighteen or nineteen, you think nothing bad can happen to you! He came overseas with the battalion as a Private First Class and rose through the ranks to Platoon Sergeant and received a Bronze star and a battlefield commission just before we arrived in January. In early January 1945, at Mageret, Belgium where both Web Halvorsen and Ray Mutz were wounded – just outside Bastogne – he assumed command of his platoon and directed the defense against a heavy counter attack by the Germans. He was known by the squad members as " the Dago ". GI's were not prone to use Army rank titles at all times.

John, and I went through the same fighting described in Peter Betchner's chapter. Several actions remain to be told. One day early in February we were across the Our river in Germany facing the Seigfied line. We were looking into concrete German bunkers about three hundred yards from a wooded area where we had dug our foxholes. Our squad was sent on a daylight patrol south toward the small German town of Dasburg. All of a sudden we were getting shelled by mortars. We jumped into shell holes and waited for the next volley. We could hear the humph, humph sound as they were fired and ten silent seconds later they exploded nearby. One soldier jumped in the shell hole with me, more scared worse than I was. He said, "The next one's coming right in this hole with us!" My reply was if it did you would never know it – as I continued reciting the first part of the 23 Psalm. Dean Adams, our Tennessee hillbilly squad member, shouted all at once, " There they are!" pointing up the hill near a hedge. There were five German soldiers directing the fire on us. We charged up the hill firing from the hip and they fled into an open field to get away – which was a fatal mistake for them. Dean probably saved us as he did several times. He had the instinct of a Tennessee squirrel hunter. It gave all of us a terrible feeling and a pause for silence.

I had written home on February 17th , " I got lost from my outfit today with my BAR teammate *(John)* and we had a dickens of a time catching up. We hopped rides with a different company and finally ended up in the right town." Since every letter was censored, we couldn't give locations. We were headed to the tiny Luxembourg town of Weicherdange where we got showers, food and clean clothes before we started out on the next offensive February 20th. We were in a brick and stone building which had been a dairy.

The 20th of February 1945 is a date which we don't forget. It was the day our 6th Armored Division broke through the Siegfried line starting with a huge artillery barrage at

6:45 AM. By the 22nd of February we were in the town of Olmscheid – 45 pillboxes were taken and 269 PW's captured. On Feb. 23rd, Combat team 50 ploughed through light opposition to take the high ground southeast of Daleiden. 252 more PW's were captured. This high ground is an interesting story about our rifle squad.

We were assigned the job of holding the high ground against a possible Nazi counterattack. Our outpost was on top of a switchback rocky road at the summit of the road to Olmscheid. We were told to expect an armored column to head over this road to attack and try to escape to the east. Our plan was to dig into the ditch on the downhill side of the road so that the enemy tank machine guns could not depress to that line of fire. As the lead tank came alongside, we were prepared to fire a rifle grenade at the track disabling it. One of us was designated to jump up on the top of the tank, open the hatch quickly dropping a grenade inside. Then we planned to open up with rifle fire as the crew bailed out if any were left. We didn't even have a bazooka with us nor any means of communication with our Company B command post.

It was freezing cold that night. My buddy, John Axelson and I had one shelter half to keep us warm. We took turns huddling on the rocky surface while our partner covered the one on the ground tightly. The one under the tarp could light a cigarette to use the heat to keep the fingers from getting too stiff to fire. We could hear the German vehicles moving below us – engines grinding away - like the vehicles were struggling in mud on the slope. Not one of us thought of leaving the outpost. We just wondered how the firefight was going to turn out hoping the advantage of surprise would be our savior. We spent the entire night in a high state of alert and frightfulness expecting at anytime German advance patrols or scout vehicles to precede the larger tanks, their engines and clanking tracks making loud noises down in the valley. Fortunately for us, the Germans elected not to go over the high road at night considering it too dangerous. Looking back, I wonder how any Commander could send out soldiers on a mission such as this without better firepower support. We were lucky again.

The 90th Infantry Division replaced us on March 4th near the German town of Schonecken. In two weeks of fighting through the Siegfried line we had advanced 13 miles in a straight line into Germany in rugged country. The 6th Armored Division was refitted, weapons cleaned, vehicles repaired and soldiers rested for another assault through the Siegfried line. We were temporarily assigned to the US 7TH Army after traveling south through France to Chateau Salins. There General Grow called the entire division together on a hillside describing our next northeast assault into Germany to meet the Third Army near the Rhine River. We crossed the Rhine at Oppenheim, advanced north toward Frankfurt , crossed the Main River near Offenbach and raced up the Autobahn toward Kassel where the First Army had trapped 300,000 Germans in the

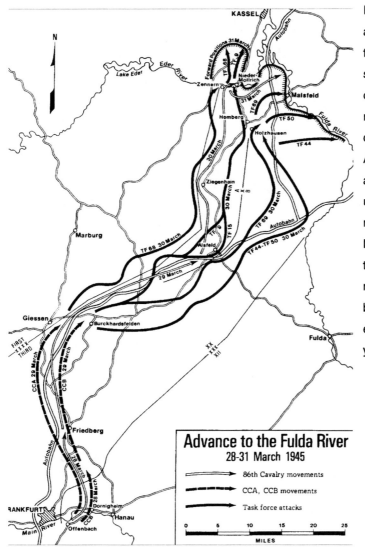

Ruhr pocket. There are many photos of this part of our drive showing thousands of German soldiers marching south in the center of the Autobahn while our armored columns are using all lanes moving north. By March 30th we thought the end was near but it is hard to believe when the enemy still shoots at you.

Map courtesy of the 6th Armored Div. Assn.- THE SUPER SIXTH -by George Hoffman 1975

On March 30th, Good Friday, we were near Kassel and on the 75 mile dash north, nine hundred Hungarian Jewish women – slave laborers at munitions plants - were liberated. Their thin skeleton like frames and tattered clothes told their story as they waved to us as we went by in our half-tracks. Maybe that's why we were fighting this war.

The 6th Armored Div. had gone right through the small German town, Zieganhain – while the German Army was collapsing. Just outside of town there was a castle on a hill. In the late 1930's it was selected as the *Fuhrerhauptquartier* with underground bunkers. Hitler was here during the invasion of the Belgium and France through the Losheim Gap in May 1940. At the start of the Battle of the Bulge on December 16,1944, it was again used as the *Oberkommandos* west headquarters of Field Marshall General Gerd von Rundstedt.

March 31st we ran into stiff resistance once again at the small town of Malsfeld, just 20 miles south of Kassel on the Fulda River. These rivers were not very wide perhaps no more than 50 -100 feet but were armor obstacles when the bridges were blown by the retreating Germans. We had tank support in this town as well as artillery. We advanced to the stone and brick buildings at the west side of the rivers edge. Germans were in the buildings on the east side. Our tanks would poke their guns around a corner of a building, fire a shot or two and then quickly back away behind a building for shelter of the deadly German 88 mm artillery. Our rifle squad was in a large stone and brick building toward the edge of town. It was part farm building and had some big grey horses in stalls in the barn part of the building. No civilians were in the area – they had fled earlier. John and I set up the BAR with the bipod in the north side of the barn door opening in the shadows. He was with Sgt. Howard Ostrom and the ammunition was at his side. The gun was not visible across the river from the German side. However the deadly muzzle flash in the shadows of the barn door opening would be visible. John and I had an agreement to not fire that weapon unless we had a good target – and then to move it as fast as possible.

They asked our squad to go up in the adjacent connected building to fire at any German soldiers and see if we could locate the German 88's that were firing at us. We carefully went from floor to floor in different windows firing at the Germans, which we could sometimes see running from buildings. We were careful to stand a yard or two behind the windows when firing to minimize muzzle flash – and then move to another location. We were afraid of showing our position, provoking a German 88 crew to fire at our window. I heard John firing the BAR when I was on the third floor. I told John Gettel, our squad Sgt. that I should go down quickly and help John move. I ran down the steps to the ground floor, got to the barn door where the grey horses were in their stall. I looked down to the end of the barn and saw John and just then heard the shell coming in. I hit the barn cobblestone floor. The horses jumped and neighed from fright. After the explosion I got up to run down toward John and Dean Adams jumped out and stopped me. He said, " Don't look, he's gone. You can't do anything! " Both John Axelson and Howard Ostrom died instantly by a direct hit. I was devastated even though we had all seen death and wounded around before.

From that point on to the end of the war on May 8,1945 our squad did not have a BAR nor did we request one from ordinance. The next day, Easter Sunday, the Germans had fled. The sun came out and it was a beautiful Spring day. Our Chaplain found a small white country church nearby and held a brief service for us and prayers for John and Howard. I remember how clean it was and the sun shone through the windows. I thought John and I were invincible. Surely, John and Howard ascended into Heaven that Easter Sunday.

Well, wars go on. They don't stop for the wounded or dead – they just plod ahead until man learns to stop killing his fellow man. If John had lived two more days, he would have reached his twentieth birthday on April 2nd. In John's last letter home he wrote, "…my plans are to go to college and be a History and Physical Education teacher." By April 17th the war was over for us – we had met the Russians. On May 19,1945 I quietly celebrated my nineteenth birthday wondering how it was that I was alive and others died or were wounded terribly.

Eva said the family received a telegram from the War Department early in April saying he was missing in action and then two weeks later received another saying he was killed in action. On Sunday June 3, 1945, the Free Church in Milaca had a memorial service for John. She said her mother cried for a year!

FREE CHURCH NEWS

In Memoriam

PFC. JOHN HOWARD AXELSON

1925 - 1945

A telegram from the War Department brought the message to the Enoch Axelson home that their son, Pfc. John Axelson, had been killed in action in Germany on March 31st. John's GOLD STAR is the first among the 43 blue stars on our Service Flag; and it is with sorrow in our hearts that we place it there. And yet, may it always be a reminder that he GAVE his life for your freedom and mine; we pray that he shall not have died in vain!

John Howard Axelson was born at McGregor, North Dakota, April 2, 1925. The family later lived in Duluth, Minnesota for a few years before moving to Milaca, Minnesota in the fall of 1932. John graduated from the Milaca High School in 1943. On July 21, 1944 he was inducted into the army, receiving his basic training in the Infantry at Camp Hood, Texas. He left for overseas duty on December 28 and was stationed in France, Luxembourg, and Germany where he served with the Sixth Armored Division of the Third Army and was killed in action on March 31, 1945. Had he lived only two days more he would have reached his 21st birthday.

He is survived by his parents and one sister, Eva, of Milaca. Other relatives and many friends join with the bereaved family in praying that this trial shall be the means of leading all who knew him to a more devoted life to the cause of righteousness and peace. May we have grace to say with Job "The Lord gave and the Lord hath taken away; blessed be the Name of the Lord."

MEMORIAL SERVICE

Sunday, June 3, 1945 at 2:30 p. m.

Prelude—"Sweet Hour of Prayer"
   Mrs. Don Sandberg, Pianist

Invocation by the Pastor

Scripture—Psalm 119:33-50

Song—"God Leads His Dear Children"
   By the FCYF Mixed Quartet

Sketch of life

Brief Talk by Mr. A. R. Cravens
   Legion Commander

Attaching the Gold Star to Flag

Taps—by Harry Bloomquist

Song—"Abide With Me" by the Quartet

Message—"When Sorrow Comes"
   By Pastor Leonard E. Hagstrom

Closing Prayer and Benediction

Postlude—"Jesus Savior Pilot Me."

THE ROD

O Thou whose sacred feet have trod
   The thorny path of woe;
Forbid that I should slight the rod,
   Or faint beneath the blow.

Give me the spirit of Thy trust,
   To suffer as a son;
To say, though lying in the dust,
   Father! Thy Will be done.
      —Selected.

"Let the words of my mouth and the meditation of my heart, be acceptable in Thy sight, O Lord, my strength, and my Redeemer"—Psalm 19:14.

WELCOME TO THE CHURCH WITH A LIVING CHRIST!

In 1947, Enoch, Esther and Eva went to Sweden with plans of going to Germany to find John's grave as originally reported.

"Dad had contact with a State Representative to help – never did learn how it happened. Shortly after arriving in Sweden, the folks received a letter that John's remains had been located and would be shipped back to the States – that was in August 1947." In August,1950, Mr. Axelson received this letter from the Department of the Army.

DEPARTMENT OF THE ARMY
OFFICE OF THE QUARTERMASTER GENERAL
WASHINGTON 25, D. C.

IN REPLY REFER TO
QMGMC 293
Axelson, John H.
SN 37 600 063

23 August 1950

Mr. Enoch Axelson
Route #3
Milaca, Minnesota

Dear Mr. Axelson:

Reference is made to the interment of your son, the late Private First Class John H. Axelson, and his comrade which was made in Grave No. 7961, Section C, Block 4, Fort Snelling National Cemetery, 7601 - 34th. Avenue, South, Minneapolis 9, Minnesota. It is regretted that because of the fact it was impossible to identify the remains of your son you were deprived of the comfort and consolation which might have been afforded by interring his remains at home.

It is felt that you might like to have the inclosed photographs of the grave and the headstone which has been erected.

You are assured that the grave will always be cared for in a manner fully commensurate with the sacrifice your son has made for his country. Any desired information concerning the grave or the cemetery will be furnished upon request.

Sincerely yours,

F. A. KIRK
Major, QMC
Memorial Division

2 Incls
    Photographs

This book is dedicated to John Howard Axelson and Howard Ostrom and all of the other thousands upon thousands of young American men – many teenagers - who didn't make it home from World War II. <u>Why</u> others of us did get home and enjoyed a good long life – we will never know! It doesn't seem fair for you to have given the ultimate sacrifice for world freedom. But, Soldiers, foxhole buddies, pals, friends we will never forget you!

John Axelson's and Howard Ostrom's Memorial marker at
Ft. Snelling, Minnesota

ABOUT THE AUTHOR

I was born May 19, 1926 in Wausau, Wisconsin, a small Midwestern town of 27,000. My parents, George Sebastian Wirth and Belle Hudson Wirth had different parentages. My father's was French and German while my mother's was English. I grew up during the Depression years graduating from Wausau High School along with 389 others on May 31, 1944 – just 7 days before D-Day. Like most young men, I was afraid the war would soon be over, so I volunteered to go into the service ahead of schedule – my neighbor was on the draft board. On August 24th I left Wausau by bus for Ft. Sheridan, Illinois, an induction center. It was exciting to become a soldier.

On September 2nd our steam train arrived at Camp Fannin, Texas near Tyler, an IRTC (infantry replacement training center). The schedule called for 17 weeks of basic training, a 2 week furlough home and then assignment to another military unit. Because of high casualty rates in Europe from D-Day on, the Army was short of two things – infantry replacements and ammunition. Secretary of War, Henry Stimson, solved the problem. Our training cycle was shortened two weeks and our two-week furlough home was reduced to a four-day delay en route to an East Coast embarkment center. I left for

Europe on the French liner, Ile de France, on January 8th 1945. By late January, the final stages of the Battle of the Bulge, I joined our rifle squad in northern Luxembourg at Kalborn, a tiny hamlet at the German border. One could look across the Our River valley (the Our River being the border) into the Siegfried line about one mile away. I didn't know a single person. I was in the same rifle squad that Ray Mutz, (wounded on Jan. 13, 1945) was in along with Peter Betchner and John Axelson who had arrived a few days before me. I thought they were all veterans – in fact we were all replacements with none having been in the squad since the 6th Armored started combat on July 27, 1944.

When the war ended on May 8th 1945, I was still 18 years old. Many of us did not have enough Army points to go home. A soldier needed 85 points to be in the first groups headed to the good old USA. Points were given for the length of time in the Army, whether you were married and had children, combat medals and campaigns etc. The 6th Armored went home, but those of us with fewer points were reassigned. I was sent to the 3rd Armored Division, as a rifleman, which was billeted in the Frankfurt, Germany area. What was the Army of Occupation like?

From July 17th to August 3rd 1945, President Harry Truman was in Potsdam, Germany (a suburb of Berlin) at the Potsdam conference with Churchill and Stalin. On one of the weekends, Harry Truman had enough of Joseph Stalin and decided to visit SHAEF headquarters in Frankfurt. The 3rd Armored Div. started polishing up for a parade for Harry. We even tried to polish our old Army shoes for the occasion. We were marched out to an airfield road waiting for all of the dignitaries. Ike was coming, along with Omar Bradley, George Patton and Courtney Hodges – all the top Generals of the US Army in Europe! Our Battalion was told to form a platoon of Missouri soldiers for President Truman – the Missouri Mules we called them. We were standing lined up at parade rest in the hot summer sun and looking down the road, we could see the red flashing lights of the parade cars. Just before the lead car reached our area, an old German woman, complete with babushka, came walking across the road from a wooded area pulling an old wooden cart loaded with forest twigs that she had picked up for fuel. Secret Service agents leaped off the running boards of the vehicles and hustled the old woman and the cart into the woods away from the Presidents cavalcade. She obviously had no idea what she interrupted. The parade went on and we got to see all the Generals and Harry Truman shake hands with the Missouri Mules.

Shortly after this I was transferred to the 1st Armored Div. when the 3rd Armored went home. My military records had been lost in the shuffle – I was a rifleman. Arriving in a small German town, Aalen, with a population of 10,000 people governed by 200 GI's, 1st Lt. Ted Rothbauer, asked me what

I did in the 6th Armored. I told him I was a jeep driver. He told me to go to the motor pool and get a jeep since I was his driver. He was a graduate of Penn State University in Animal Husbandry and his job was to drive to Berlin about once per month to make certain that the Berlin populace was not drinking milk contaminated by tuberculin disease. So, I got to see Berlin or what was left of it. The Reichstag area was completely devastated. SHAEF headquarters along with General Eisenhower moved to Berlin. On one trip during the winter, I was waiting for Lt. Ted in a temporary building outside of headquarters. A beautiful brunette WAC Captain came into the shed along with a Scotty dog. She asked the dispatcher for a jeep driver to take her to her billet. There weren't any available. When she turned to me, I explained that I was not from headquarters and I was waiting for Lt. Ted. But, I quickly changed my mind and told her to hop in my jeep. She introduced herself as Capt. Kay Summersby, Gen. Eisenhower's private secretary. She had to hurry home to prepare for a big party that night at headquarters. When I got back, Lt. Ted was waiting for me in the shack so I had some explaining to do. We always stayed in Reichsminister Funk's home in the suburb of Wannsee – taken over as hotel for field grade officers and above. I stayed in the basement since I was a Pfc., with the Sergeant in charge of the building!

We were paid in German Occupation marks as were all of the four nation Allied soldiers, Americans, British, French and the Russians. Each army had a different code before the script money number so that American marks were only good in the American PX's and their sector of Germany. The Russian soldiers were paid at the end of the war – for four years - with absolute nothing but junk to buy in Berlin. A German lady in the Potsdammer Platz sold pot menders to lines of Russian soldiers for 50 cents equivalent in marks. What could they do with pot menders? Somehow an American officer, as a paymaster, made the mistake of paying a whole division of American soldiers in Russian coded marks. That opened the flood-gate, as now all marks of all the four countries were legal tender. Inflation accelerated. Cigarettes became the common currency. GI's rations were two cartons per week at their PX for 50 cents per carton. In Europe everyone wanted American cigarettes. In Berlin, the Russians paid $135 per carton for Chesterfields and Lucky Strikes and $200 per carton for the longer Pall Mall's. Elsewhere in Germany you could trade four cartons of cigarettes for a Leica camera.

I got to travel Europe in late 1945 and early 1946 – to Paris, Versailles, the Riviera, a one week ski trip for $85 at Zermatt, Switzerland and of course all the major cities in Germany. Most of my soldier friends were always broke spending their $85 per month soldiers pay, so three of my trips were those turned down by other soldiers. It was an education for a nineteen year old from northern Wisconsin.

My discharge papers show that I departed from Europe (via Liberty ship from LeHavre) on 17 Jun 46 and was separated from the Army 9 Jul 46 from Ft. Sheridan, Illinois. I was credited with one year, 5 months and 19 days of <u>foreign service</u>.

When I got off the Hiawatha train in Wausau, Wisconsin, my mother greeted me and said, " you are going to Carleton College this Fall!" She had enrolled me while I was in Germany. I spent four wonderful years at this Northfield, Minnesota college graduating with a BA degree in Economics in 1950. I knew my future wife, Marjorie Christiansen, at Carleton but we did not date until we were both out of school. We were married in 1952. We have two children, son, Scott and daughter, Carol and two grandchildren. Our whole family attended the final reunion of the 6th Armored Division in Louisville, Kentucky in September, 2000. I had a career in the investment business as a stockbroker in Chicago on LaSalle Street. Through the years I have been active in YMCA activities and have been especially privileged to renew acquaintances with my Army friends of the past with whom we have an unusual bond of friendship! We know we don't have much time left to record our World War II experiences for future historians.

Bibliography

Adolph Hitler	John Toland
Ardennes – the Secret War	Charles Whiting
As You Were Soldier	Col. James Moncrief
August 1944 – the Campaign For France	Robert A. Miller
Band of Brothers E Co. 506th Regt.	
Of the 101st Airborne	Stephan E. Ambrose
Bastogne	Guy Franz Arend
Battle: the Story of the Bulge	John Toland
The Battle of the Huertgen Forest	Charles Whiting
Beyond the Beachhead – the 29th Infantry	
Division in Normandy	Joseph Balkowski
The Bitter Woods – the Battle of the Bulge	John S.D. Eisenhower
A Blood Dimmed Tide	Gerald Astor
Closing With the Enemy	Michael D. Doubler
Combat History of the Super Sixth	Sixth Armored Division
Crusade in Europe	Dwight D. Eisenhower
Dark December	Robert E. Merriam
The Day the War Ended	Martin Gilbert
D-Day June 6, 1944	Stephan E. Ambrose
D-Day and the Invasion of Normandy	Anthony Kemp
Decision in Normandy	Carlo D'Este
Dresden - the Devils Tinderbox	Alexander McKee
Eisenhower	Stephan E. Ambrose
Eisenhower	David Eisenhower
Eisenhower's Lieutenants	Russell F. Weigley
Final Entries 1945 – the Diaries of	
Joseph Goebbels	Hugh Trevor
Hitler's Germany	Bernt Englemann
Hitler's Last Gamble –	
The Battle of the Bulge	Trevor N. Dupuy
Hitler's War	David Irving
The Last Assault – 1944 the Battle of	
The Bulge Reassessed	Charles Whiting
Le Panzer De Peiper	Gerard Gregoire
The Malmedy Massacre	John Bauserman
The Memoirs of Field Marshall Keitel	Field Marshal Keitel
The Men of Bastogne	Fred MacKenzie
Panzer	Roger Edwards
Patton's Gap	Maj. Gen. Richard Rohmer
Patton & His Third Army	Gen. Brenton G. Wallace
Patton's Third Army at War	George Forty
Pattern of Circles – an Ambassador's Story	John E. Dolobois
The Rise and Fall of the Third Reich	William L. Shirer
Siegfried – the Nazis Last Stand	Charles Whiting
Spearhead in the West – History	
Of the Third Armored Division	Col. John A. Smith, Jr.

A Time For War – Franklin D. Roosevelt
And the Path To Pearl Harbor   *Robert Smith Thompson*

A Time For Trumpets   *Charles B. MacDonald*
To Save Bastogne – the 110th Inf. Regt.
Of the 28th Infantry Division   *Robert F. Phillips*
War As I Knew It   *Gen. George S. Patton, Jr*
-Cover Photo-
"Blaine Harbor Sunset" (8/3/2000)   *Brian Arthur Blevins*